The Crisis of Desire

The Crisis of Desire

....

AIDS AND THE FATE
OF GAY BROTHERHOOD

....

Robin Hardy

WITH DAVID GROFF

....

MI
IN
NE
SO
TA

University of Minnesota Press

MINNEAPOLIS • LONDON

Copyright 1999 by the Estate of Robin Hardy

Reprinted by special arrangement with Houghton Mifflin Company

First University of Minnesota Press edition 2002

Published by the University of Minnesota Press
111 Third Avenue South, Suite 290
Minneapolis, MN 55401-2520
http://www.upress.umn.edu

A Cataloging-in-Publication record for this book is available
from the Library of Congress.

ISBN 0-8166-3911-6

Printed in the United States of America on acid-free paper

The University of Minnesota is an equal-opportunity educator and employer.

12 11 10 09 08 07 06 05 04 03 02   10 9 8 7 6 5 4 3 2 1

TO CHRISTOPHER HARDY

and to the brotherhood
engaged against AIDS

Fare forward

CONTENTS

INTRODUCTION

"Words Where There Was Silence"

ON OCTOBER 20, 1995, Robin Hardy sat down at his table in his adobe house in Tucson and wrote his last letter. He was telling his agent that he had sent his editor half the manuscript of his book about gay men and AIDS. Now he would take a break and withdraw into the desert. "I'm going camping with a friend for a few days next week," he wrote. "The nights will be cold, but the days warm for hiking, and apparently the remote canyon holds Indian ruins, maybe petroglyphs. Actually, the nights will be freezing. After about the third day I feel like I've dropped onto another planet."

Lover of men, thinker, contrarian, and activist, Robin Hardy was an HIV-positive gay man and thus already lived on another planet. Through the first half of the 1990s, he had watched his T-cell levels slide into the danger range at the same time that the machinery of AIDS treatment, safer-sex education, public concern and charity, activism, and gay male morale all appeared to collapse into exhaustion. The guerrilla warfare on his immune system laid siege to his survival. The nation's lethally laconic response to AIDS stirred his indignation. His gay brothers had been ignored, patronized, fragmented, and dispirited. Provoked by his own prospective fate, in that dark time when our drugs and our energy had failed us, he was writing furiously and richly about the implications of the virus that, he said, "ticks, a silent time bomb in my veins."

Robin would die before that bomb could explode or be defused. Adventurer that he was, he would depart adventurously. *The Crisis of Desire*, a book about the strained brotherhood of gay men in the age of AIDS, would be his parting shot and gift.

Robin Hardy left behind more than two hundred pages of his manuscript, which I have edited, updated, and elaborated upon. While he was alive, he was more than happy to offer his friends a guided tour of the landscape of his beliefs. I had to navigate on my own the paths I recall from him and venture down others for the first time, looking for Robin's footprints.

The body of this book remains intimately connected to the body of the man. Robin's presence always added voltage to his ideas and vision. Even his features were extraordinary. Robin's irises were piercingly blue, the whites around them so expansive that he looked at once fierce and startled, both predator and prey. His nose turned up a little, like Socrates'. His smile was ready and broad. He wore his chestnut hair unfashionably long, as if in homage to the Radical Faeries whose naturist gay spirituality he admired.

Though Robin was not an easy man, he was easily male. That was part of what drew many of us to him — the sense of masculine legitimacy he radiated. Gay men often wear their queer bodies with tentativeness and studied formality, like tuxedos to be returned to the rental shop. Robin inhabited his body like an old pair of jeans. Through some genetic gift and psychic hard work, he had come to trust his body and relish it. His physique was not regulation (little about Robin was ever regulation). He was a little thick in places. He slouched. Though he could dress up as well as the next boy, his clothes often had holes, and his pants drooped. He wasn't butch, nor exactly did he act like a straight man. Robin could camp with the best of them — and he had a pointed wit, often sharpened with indignation.

His mind and maleness arrested me the moment I met him. In November 1988 I was a guest at a New York party hosted by George Stambolian, a French professor at Wellesley who had helped legitimatize gay male fiction through his *Men on Men* anthologies. I had a story in the most recent collection. I looked up to see a tall man framed against George's doorway, grinning. His name was Robin — not Robert, *Robin*. He was a writer, journalist, and editor. In the following weeks I made sure we spent a great deal of time together. One night I invited him to a publishing party hosted by Eric Ashworth, the gay literary agent who would die of AIDS in August 1997. At one point, as we leaned head-to-head over the hors d'oeuvres table, our hair fell across our respective foreheads and touched. A spark shot through me.

We went out drinking afterward at a neighborhood bar, Chelsea Transfer. Robin and I had the kind of significant-sounding, heady conversation that you have when someone new excites you and scares you. I would ask him questions — about his native Canada, his writing, his trips to Europe, his experiences with boyfriends. Robin kept his story in the shadows, allowing few glimpses into the inner man. He was working-class, he said, almost belligerently. He had left his family home early. He had lived with a woman. He had gone to law school. He was clearly proud of being Canadian and liked the acute angle on America that his nationality provided him. He had written for the *Body Politic* in Toronto — did I know what that was? "You have to read this booklet, *With Downcast Gays*," he told me. "It's the most important writing about gay male sexuality ever published." He had spent much time in Europe, and some time on Anna Maria Island off the Gulf Coast of Florida, where a heron had once strolled into his living room.

He worked for a small book-packaging house as an editor, and he wrote male adventure fiction and Hardy Boys novels, none of them under his own name. One Hardy boy creating other Hardy boys, Robin clearly enjoyed infusing the most hetero of adventure stories with the subversive smoke of homoeroticism.

Over the next months we would become friends. Slowly, he would allow me enough flashes of light to assemble his character in all its contradictions. I soon learned how fierce his vision was and how unwilling he could be to compromise. His absolutism would frustrate me. He saw betrayal everywhere. Yet there was something nearly boyish in his appetite for battle; it was at once disconcerting and infectious. His passions were something his friends would have to live up to and live down. Tragic, silly, or infuriating, for me he would remain as physical as earth.

Robin Hardy came to AIDS as a lifelong witness to chronic disease. As he describes in *The Crisis of Desire*, his two brothers were born with cystic fibrosis, a genetically inherited disease of the exocrine glands that usually kills by the end of childhood. Robin was spared the collusion of genes that kick-starts cystic fibrosis. But he watched with a child's alertness his brothers' struggle for breath. Though he would not speak of it in detail to many of his friends, the experience of chronic disease influenced him enormously. He could not but feel guilt at his dumb luck in being born healthy. He may even have felt extra responsibility to live more fully on his brothers' behalf. He certainly learned what it means to wage war for command of your body.

Cystic fibrosis told Robin that if you wanted to stay alive you had to oppose a system — not only the workings of an illness that would rack your body, but the machinations of health care and government. Most of all you had to contest the prescriptions and prognoses issued to you. To keep itself inured from your doom, the world had established a set of myths you were expected to fulfill — namely, that your role was to struggle manfully and then die. Only by contesting the world's expectations could you persist in living.

Having an obdurate illness meant striving against the prevailing winds. For Robin, to survive — as his brother Christopher did for so long, and as his brother Charles continues to do — was to challenge not just fate but fatalism.

When Christopher Hardy died in late 1984 at age thirty-four, he was one of Canada's oldest living survivors of cystic fibrosis. Robin had come home from traveling in Europe and America to help nurse his brother into death. In the following months, as AIDS gave him new reasons to grieve, Robin would confront this new disease from a distinct perspective. Over the next ten years he would accumulate the rest of the experiences and insights, angers and griefs, that shape this book. Challenging AIDS and its myths came to dominate his life.

After Christopher's death he moved to New York City, which by the mid-1980s was barely recognizable as the birthplace of the Stonewall rebellion, the 1969 uprising against corrupt and antigay police that was the opening event of contemporary lesbian and gay culture. It is almost impossible to overstate how hopelessly dark gay life became when the epidemic first took hold. The gay men who had come together for the first Christopher Street Liberation Day gay pride marches, had danced at the Flamingo and populated Fire Island, and redefined what male sexuality could be, now stood waiting for the next time bomb to explode. For a long time, before the virus that causes AIDS was identified, every kind of intimate contact was suspect, and disaster could strike you, your lover, or your best friend like sniper fire. Sex, which had seemed the portal into a new way of bonding among men — indeed, for people of all sexualities — now, it seemed, caused cancer. That was an outlandish notion in 1986. With the closing of bathhouses and back rooms, sex had at best been domesticated and at worst suffused with fear. When the inevitability and enormity of AIDS became evident, gay men found that their personal meaning arose not from their physical promise but from how they operated the machinery of sickness and dying. They buddied the sick, exchanged the folklore of alternative medicines, memorialized the dead. The Stonewall-era vocation was shouldered aside by a minimal, elemental aspiration: the cessation of pain and death.

Compounding the diurnal disasters was the profound isolation many gay men felt. Having been marginalized and scorned when they came out as gay, they were pariahs for new reasons now, both ignored and vilified by much of the mainstream establishment. The American government initially offered little money and less interest in AIDS. Moreover, by the late 1980s, when HIV antibody testing became commonplace, gay men found themselves separating into two camps, the antibody-positive and antibody-negative — those who it seemed were fated to develop AIDS and those who were exempted. HIV apartheid, which persists today, was a further trauma to the unifying bond of sexuality forged since Stonewall.

By 1990 Robin Hardy had lost several lovers, numerous friends in New York, Canada, and France, many of his gay liberation friends associated with the *Body Politic*, and two psychotherapists. He had also discovered he was HIV-positive himself, which gave him more than a mourner's interest in what AIDS did to human bodies. As someone who had lived on two continents, written about gay male identity in two countries, and watched his brother's death, he had no choice but to face AIDS eye to eye. What would be demanded of gay men, he asked, if they and their tribe were to survive this viral and cultural cataclysm?

Like many gay men in New York, San Francisco, and other cities, Robin would join ACT UP, the AIDS Coalition to Unleash Power, founded in March 1987 by a group of long-time activists mobilized around AIDS, their private grief politicizing into fury. As it grew more visible, ACT UP would set an agenda not just for activists but for gay men of many different stripes. The group's slogans, distinctive urban-guerrilla style, and fractious solidarity allowed them to claim a new identity. Robin participated in the "Stop the Church" march on St. Patrick's Cathedral on December 8, 1989, protesting Cardinal John O'Connor's refusal to allow condom distribution in New York City public schools. In theory, ACT UP was tailored for Robin Hardy. Its radical, prosexual passion complemented his own ideology and temperament. Still, Robin swiftly grew impatient with the group's mercurial impulses and lugubrious deliberations. He was not cut out to work with other people in groups. Later, when he was cochair of the gay and lesbian publishing network group the Publishing Triangle, his grand plans would have required the group to have as many members and as much force of will as a small army. Robin brought a joi de vivre to the Triangle, but he was a bull in a rare-editions shop. He was meant to be yelling in the streets and handing out leaflets, buttonholing bystanders, haranguing the foot soldiers, pointing to the big picture.

Robin would make his major contribution through his critical writing. His magazine and newspaper journalism would focus on several areas of concern: the need to challenge established notions of AIDS treatment and activism; the right of the dying to die; the need to take command of the stories being told about AIDS; and the future of gay male desire.

Robin wrote several influential articles in the *Village Voice* about public gay male sexuality that formed the early draft of a chapter in *The Crisis of Desire*. New forms of homoerotic sexual expression arose in the rubble of 1980s gay sexuality, focusing around safe-sex clubs and the joys of mutual masturbation. Robin found great significance in the dark but surprisingly cheerful corridors of these clubs, where gay men won a reprieve from disease and even from the need to be particular. You could set aside your own story, which might be shot through with grief or fear, and string a connection between yourself and other men, and you could do so without fear of contagion.

Robin Hardy would not deny the risks of gay men connecting physically in groups, nor would he see such activity as the only sexual vocation a gay man could have. He knew the dangers of sexual addiction, and he was aware of how easy it could be for some men to avoid intimacy by having sex with a lot of other men. Nor did he deny the epidemiological dangers multipartner sex might provide, especially when the clubs began to encourage more sexually risky sex acts. He was in favor of male-male relationships, but broadly defined. Romantic life was another myth that gay men too easily swallowed. He looked fiercely askance at the reflex to venerate monogamy as the great gay sociosexual good. But in the harsh landscape of death, gay warriors were building tribal campfires, sexual circles providing warmth and light. He saw gay men not just getting off but getting together, engaged in a primal connection central to the functioning of the tribe and the spiritual calling of gay men. For Robin, sexual desire was the electricity that bonded us like brothers.

AIDS is not a "gay disease" — or so we have been told, by both straight and gay media and activists. Because it could strike anybody, everybody should care about it. This idea made Robin very angry. Gay men have always formed the majority of those infected and affected by HIV, yet homosexuals have repeatedly been shoved to the background of the AIDS group picture. Foregrounded were the numerically sparse but highly sympathetic faces of Republican women, white schoolkids, and cute babies of all colors, who plucked at the hearts of straight journalists and the pockets of politicians. Gay men have been perceived as mindlessly promiscuous infectious agents whose viral illnesses, if left uncontained, could seep into the precious "general population."

Seeking to be positively included in the AIDS saga, gay men willingly neutered and sweetened themselves. Their characters would become as two-dimensional as the names they stitched onto the AIDS quilt. In mainstream newspaper features, plays, and eventually movies and television, mothers were substituted for lovers and gay men appeared as waifs, prodigal sons accepted by their families when they came home, gaunt, denuded of desire, and ready to die. What mattered, of course, was not the fate of gay men themselves, but the reactions they stirred in straight people. Robin would seethe whenever he read another newspaper story about how, say, rich people coped when their AIDS-ridden decorator dropped dead mid-project. Every personal testament of a heterosexual woman ponderously getting tested for HIV would leave him disturbed and furious, not for what the story said but for what it omitted.

The government's laggard response to AIDS and the confused and bureaucratic research and treatment efforts were, to him, less a result of a broad-ranging political conspiracy than evidence of the malign neglect of gay men, who, along with people of color, the poor, and injection drug users, were at best afterthoughts in the national consciousness. If AIDS had initially affected American Legionnaires, then scientists and government officials would have scrambled to supply money, care, and fast-track treatments. AIDS was just the most convincing equation in the long proof that gay men were essentially society's orphans. Now they had become "sexual criminals," Robin said, and even worse, they reminded people that death happened.

As Robin would agree, those sentimental TV movies featuring large-eyed heterosexual children did their work as propaganda. The AIDS quilt not only memorialized the dead but pried hearts open. What got Robin was how gay men had to proceed from a position of abasement. Having long been the flower arrangers, nurses, teachers, and service providers of the dominant culture, they were primed to approach AIDS like supplicants, uncertain of their own power, relying on the kindness of strangers and the unearned emotion of sentimentality. "Someday," Robin told me, "I'm going to write an essay called 'The Homosexual as Poodle.' "

Robin also worried that the reflex to plead would bruise gay men's relationships with other groups affected by AIDS as we all struggled for money and attention from the communications industry and the government. In the *Voice*, he would write angrily about how in the AIDS movement itself the needs of seropositive gay men were often subsumed by the broader agenda of people not infected by HIV who, in their fight for national health insurance or abortion rights, had the advantage of time. Those were vital causes, Robin believed, but they were less immediate concerns than the untended international emergency of AIDS. Prevalent in ACT UP and in other AIDS activist organizations was what Robin would call, in the *Village Voice*, "an attitude of self-abnegation which subordinates gay identity to the political agendas of absentee allies."

Robin's article caused an uproar when it was published in 1991. Robin could seem uncaring about nongay people with AIDS, but this was not the case; he was writing out of his fear that AIDS would destroy gay identity. To hear that the pink triangle might be removed from ACT UP's banner spurred Robin to feel how not only their enemies but their allies could disempower gay men.

Robin cared about how his gay brothers lived and also how they died. In 1990 he went to Amsterdam to witness — participate in — the death of one of his lovers, a man named Hans Faasse. Hans was one of the many men who had made up Robin's European fraternity, men who approached living from the oblique, subversive angle that Robin relished. Like many gay men, Robin had relationships that were intermittent yet intense, mysterious, and deep. Hans, Robin's long-time, peripatetic companion, was wearied and thinned by his battle with AIDS and had decided to die.

Euthanasia is legal in the Netherlands; the medical establishment even has set a standard of terminal care that eases dying. Hans created a departure for himself that was both harrowing and sustaining for those who witnessed it. For Robin, Hans's death was transformative. Returning from Amsterdam, he talked about it incessantly, in moment-by-moment detail as we had dinner one cold night in Greenwich Village. He led me to his walkup on Bleecker Street so that I could see a videotape he had made of Hans's last days.

I watched with discomfort and fear as Hans said goodbye and disappeared into his bedroom with a shot glass of phenobarbital his doctor had supplied. As Robin saw it, Hans had been able to listen to his own body, say goodbye to his friends, come to terms with the fact of his impending death, and plan his exit. Few of us, gay or straight, have any say in when or how we die. AIDS has made that very clear. Yet at a time when gay men felt powerless over their fates, Hans had retained mastery over his departure.

Having grown up in a family where death could descend at any time, Robin appreciated how Hans could decide the means and the date of his dying. But I think another element in Hans's way of death also appealed to Robin. He did not die on his own. The state helped him; doctors eased his way. American gay men were getting sick and dying while estranged from the national systems of research, treatment, and even disposal — witness the number of men shipped home to expire among families they had long since left behind, men who had little say about the circumstances of their own demise. Hans died surrounded by friends and lovers. The state, like a caring and sensible parent, had come to his aid. That parent could not save his life, but it could wipe his brow. Hans's death spoke not just to Robin the angry, pro-euthanasia activist; it appealed as well to the wayward son. Unlike most gay men, Hans was able to die accepted and cared about not just by his lovers but by his country. If he had to die, at least he died within a loving fraternity. Even an AIDS death could provide a vision for how things might change. As Robin writes in *The Crisis of Desire*, "Gay men made dying gay."

The death of Hans, his writing about AIDS, and the state of his own health — all these factors would combine to change the terms of

Robin's life in the 1990s. He withdrew into greater solitude even as he came to connect himself further with his family and his gay identity. His romantic life remained a puzzle; I could never figure out the pattern among the men he dated. A lot of men made their way through his life, some of them sex partners and some not, with many of them part of Robin's worldwide network. My favorite of Robin's houseguests was the English writer and porn star Aiden Shaw. He and the rest of Robin's men had in common their subversive grins, their subtly aggressive, bad-boy sexuality, and their near-doggish absorption in the doings of their own bodies. That is probably what Robin liked about them.

During the summer of 1990, Robin and I took shares in a little house in Fire Island Pines, a small resort about fifty miles from New York City, the only place in the world where gay men make up the vast majority of the inhabitants, at least on summer weekends. It was a community populated with contradictions — safer-sex parties hosted as benefits for an AIDS organization; a Morning Party held that year at a beachfront house by Gay Men's Health Crisis, until a thunderstorm washed the party out and consigned the drugged revelers to the Pavilion, the local dance hall, awash in mud; and, of course, the relentless presence of HIV, apparent in bodies, unspoken of except in intimate conversations, and recalled by the ghosts of dead men who populated the place more thoroughly than those of us renting. Having lived in so many places and been so long on his own, Robin could keep himself at one amused remove from the hothouse dramas that consumed the rest of us. In his writing, the Pines became one more arena where the post-Stonewall legacy of gay male sexual culture would, or would not, survive a generation wracked by AIDS.

Back in New York City, Robin left his job at the book-packaging company and went out on his own as a writer, with a contract to write Hardy Boys books and horror novels for young readers. He was more preoccupied with AIDS than ever, and more despairing too, as the AIDS activist groups began to fragment, the virus proved itself more intractable, and gay men settled into the grind of what promised to be a decades-long epidemic. His health was also causing him more concern than I realized. Thanks to his experience with cystic fibrosis, he resisted the standard treatment course for HIV and, through trial and error, laid out his own. He remained a loud proponent of captaining your own body, doing what you think is right and not what the medical people reflexively tell you to do. Basically asymptomatic, except for some skin conditions that signified lowered immunity, and rightfully dubious of the efficacy of antivirals like AZT that were being prescribed even for healthy HIV-positive people, Robin monitored his immune system carefully and was open to using new medications if his T-cell levels sank into the red zone. For all his Radical Faerie spirituality and medical contrariness, he was not an evangelist for alternative and unapproved treatments. But he did believe that real medical progress would most likely not come from the sluggish and grandiose ocean liners that were Western medical research institutions, like the National Institutes of Health, or from pharmaceutical companies, which balked at making AIDS drugs affordable and often would not favor a promising drug over a currently profitable one until conscience morphed into business imperative. The breakthroughs would come from the network of people with AIDS.

Though he kept his eye out for all kinds of medications and new protocols, he was holding out with one big hope: the AIDS vaccine. Robin believed that only a vaccine suitable for people who already had HIV would stop the epidemic in its tracks. Such a vaccine remains only an aspiration.

Once Robin borrowed eight hundred dollars from me to make a quarterly medical insurance payment. I was unnerved, for his sake, that he was living so close to the margin. He was reliant on his own efforts to support himself; he had no money or savings to fall back on. What would happen to him if he got sick? Would he turn to his ragtag collection of friends? Would he return to Canada?

In the spring of 1991 Robin told me he was moving to Tucson. He had some writer friends there he could stay with until he got started, and he had gotten reacquainted with family living in New Mexico. His New York apartment was too cramped to work in. The city was full of ghosts. Besides, he told me, "it's not safe to live in New York anymore." He didn't mean muggings. Tuberculosis bacilli were everywhere, on toilet seats and elevator buttons, in the breath of subway crowds. Some of the microbe strains were drug-resistant. It just might save his life to leave.

I was upset less by the news of his departure than by the fact that he was so worried about his health. The tuberculosis threat was very real in New York and especially fearsome for a man who had watched his brother die coughing. Suddenly Robin seemed prone to mortality.

We met for a farewell drink at Chelsea Transfer. Robin had a parting gift, something he had found while packing up his apartment. From around his neck he took a thick silver chain. "Aiden Shaw left this behind," he told me. "I'm sure he would want you to have it." I made the appropriate grateful noises, telling Robin that any item that had come in contact with the sweat molecules of Aiden Shaw was something I wanted close to my own skin. But I was thinking also of the contact the necklace had with Robin. I slipped it around my neck.

Robin liked Tucson and accomplished a lot there. In addition to his adventure-boy writing, he was also editing manuscripts for a series of young-adult biographies of major gay and lesbian figures, past and present. In the fall of 1993 I visited him. He seemed glad to have the company, and showed off his adopted desert city to me with all the possessive pride I'd seen him apply to Canada. After driving me past a graveyard for decommissioned military jets that amused him, he led me back to his little home at the end of a dusty lane. Near the edge of the real, unirrigated desert, it was a genuine adobe house, stolid and pink, sitting like an ancient painted desert lady among brilliant flowers. A veranda ran the width of the house's far side, hung with plants. Chaparral gave the place a smoky fragrance. Inside, the house was dark, tiled, and cool, the walls between rooms twelve inches of coarse adobe. The kitchen alone would have swallowed most Manhattan one-bedrooms. Robin had picked up some beat-up Mission furniture, its leather leaking stuffing. A long table stretched along one wall, with all the papers from Robin's projects spread out on it, together with notes written in his loopy, surprisingly boyish hand.

His life in Tucson seemed almost monastic, centered around a few friends, his work, and his pleasure in the desert. Evident in him was a new generosity. He seemed more measured, even muted, moving through his own thinking with greater assurance. Which is not to say he could not summon up his usual anger. He fulminated against an editor in New York who he felt had done him wrong. He spoke with both anger and sadness about the damaged physical environment in Tucson, how greedy farmers had sucked the rivers dry, leaving them unnatural arroyos all year long.

He reserved his richest fury for the local AIDS establishment. Just as he had in New York, Robin had plunged into AIDS in Arizona. Tucson, he thought, was awash in complacency. Medical people were not aggressively treating their patients; they were content to use standard medications in standard ways. "We're written off as soon as we walk in the door," he told me. Poor people, especially poor people of color, and also most gay men, accepted this casual care without a protest, as if this were all they deserved. They were not the pilots of their own health. Some accepted an AIDS diagnosis as death. Taking the initiative, Robin had successfully urged AIDS officials in Tucson to fly in Martin Delaney from Project

Inform in San Francisco. Delaney could impart fresh treatment information and an attitude of hope — that people with AIDS actually might have some say in the disposition of their lives. Robin was pleased that after hearing Delaney, some men seemed startled into hopefulness.

As he was making dinner for me that first night, Robin rinsed the salad greens under the tap and then reached under the sink to pull up a bottle of household bleach. He opened the bottle and poured a capful right into the greens, tossed them twice more, and then rinsed them again. Robin looked over at me, laughed, and shrugged. "AIDS precaution," he said. "If your immune system isn't good, you don't want any stray microbes in your raw food." I was taken aback that a man so seemingly robust was nagged with precautions like this. Moments later he was telling me that for a while the previous year he had taken an antidepressant. "The drug didn't keep me from feeling bad," he said. "But what it did was give me a bottom, so that I knew I could fall only so far." That also shocked me; Robin had always seemed too headlong to be tripped up by sadness, too intent on striding ever to fall.

Robin was coming closer to his own family, both in New Mexico, where he had visited, and in Canada, cementing himself with his parents and siblings as the turmoil around Christopher's death subsided. His absence of a network of friends worried me. I wondered how he would support himself if he got sick — I was remembering the eight-hundred-dollar insurance loan he'd needed — and who would take care of him. To my surprise, he said he might go back to Canada. The Canadian health care system was good. His family could care for him.

That night over dinner, he told me for the first time about the man he thought had infected him in West Berlin ten years before. He sounded amused, even wistful, as he related to me with relish how hot the man was — how in his nasty-boy, subversive way he had quite literally threatened Robin's life during sex. That little dance with death made the coitus even sweeter, especially in retrospect. I could see that this episode was part of some bigger story Robin had to tell; indeed, his encounter in West Berlin forms the basis of one of the most affecting passages in *The Crisis of Desire*.

In his little southwestern adobe monastery Robin was a man happy to wander his own wilderness for a time. In the midst of his anger and fear was renewed meditation. He was gathering together the strings of the stories and arguments that would become the web of this book.

In the spring of 1994 at the publishing house where I worked, I received a thick package from a literary agent containing Robin Hardy's proposal for a book about gay men and AIDS. I recognized a lot of the ideas that I'd heard Robin arguing through at writers' conferences and dinner tables. But much of the material was new to me. I had never heard many of the stories he was telling about his family and his experiences as a gay man, from the details of his brother's death to his relationship with porn auteur Arthur Bressan to the myths around sex, disease, and survival that informed the lives of contemporary gay men in plague time. I had never known the depth of Robin's losses or recognized the skein of anger and elegy he had woven around them. I admired too how his thesis was not limited to AIDS but used the disease as a point of entry into the existential concerns arising around life, death, and human connection. Reacting to the work of such defiantly opinionated AIDS writers as Randy Shilts and Larry Kramer, but very different from them, Robin aimed to become one of the defining voices of the HIV epidemic. He would explain to us the conspiracy of benign neglect that killed so many for so long. He would give a historical and human context for HIV. And he would be a crystallizing, legitimizing voice for those gay men who had grown estranged from their selves, their stories, and their sexuality.

As it happened, another editor at another house won the right to

publish the book. So it seemed once more that I would be kibitz-
ing Robin from the sidelines, listening to his tales and screeds over
dinner and via telephone from Tucson and during his visits to
New York. When he was in town he stayed with me, his big frame
sprawled on the futon in my living room, his feet sticking out from
under the quilt. He gave me a copy of the first young-adult horror novel he had written under his own name. He dedicated the
book to "Nana Hardy, matriarch of a great northern clan, on her
ninetieth birthday," which suggests he had grown more preoccupied with his family. *Call of the Wendigo* featured an indigenous
Canadian-bred monster complete with antlers and a heart of ice.
Always a man with an agenda, Robin wanted to popularize a specifically North American mythic beast. Always subversive, he threw
in among the teenage angst and horror a few homoerotic touches.
One girl attends the Willa Cather School and dines out at the Universal Grill, whose eponym was for many years the real-life lair of
highly dramatic New York homosexuals. Though the book was very
much an entertainment, Robin took very seriously the sort of intentions and implications it represented. Later, in a Guggenheim
Foundation grant application, as he described the novel he wanted
to write, Robin said, "When I teach genre fiction at writing workshops or universities, I suggest that fiction comprises the 'dreaming'
of America; that material historical conditions engender the cycli-
cal popularity of genres, and over time, the evolution of formulas
and the creation of entirely new genres. As civilization enters a
post-modern era, I argue that the need for new mythologies to express the anomie and alienation of contemporary American lives
cannot be met by old European myths, or those we have inherited
from antiquity." How were we trapped by old myths? Where could
new ones come from? These questions preoccupied him throughout his work on what would become *The Crisis of Desire.*

Whether declaiming to his friends or sitting before the computer screen, Robin was working on his AIDS book, slowly but

surely, synthesizing the results of his unsentimental education. He maintained his secluded life. He received visits from his New York literary friends Michael Denneny and Philip Gefter and even drove to California with Philip, a trip that would cement their relationship. Robin would later boast that he had brought to Tucson two of the most seminal leaders in the gay freedom movement: Harry Hay, the founder of the Mattachine Society in the 1940s, and his lover, John Burnside. Robin loved Hay's declaration that gay men were completely different from straight people except for what they did in bed.

He grew even more connected with the desert. In a letter to Mitchell Ivers, an editor friend in New York, he wrote in droll detail of how he could and could not connect with the larger rhythms of the landscape — in this instance, the Gila Wilderness of New Mexico.

> One evening, sitting on a rock in the river with water burbling over me, wondering why we can't simply will ourselves to be permanently lost in such a paradisiacal state of nature, I was reminded of my contact lenses, the pills I take every day to stay alive, despite five days growth of whiskers, the remnants of an expensive New York haircut. In this idyll, I reflected, Jean-Jacques Rousseau meets Maxfield Parrish.

The desert also resonated with Robin's own existential perspective:

> There's very clearly a difference between an overnight or weekend camping trip, and taking six days to travel deep into a remote wilderness, where each day takes you farther and farther from human signs and artifacts. The mind slows down and empties; the body becomes an extension of soil, water, fauna and rock, sun and air. Amid a wilderness that has taken eons to form, and that will survive beyond us, for eons to come (presumably), I find a delicious sense of my own insignificance; a sense too of the transience of human troubles.

Robin goes on to ask Mitchell, an expert on Broadway, about the sexual motives of post–World War II gay men creating work for the

New York theater. "I think it would be a plangent example of the subtle connection between homoeroticism and the circuses of middle America. Like a drum, or a heart, beating beneath the garden."

"I write about the difference between words and action," Robin told his publisher on October 18, 1995, when he sent in the first completed chapters of his book, "between what our society says out loud and what we keep silent; what structuralists might refer to as the difference between discourse and behavior. . . . It is this gap between 'things as we like to believe them' and 'things as they really affect individuals' that I have been trying to bridge; to put words where our society prefers silence."

Over the summer of 1995 Robin had accomplished a lot. During a visit to New York in April, he suffered a bout of sulfa-drug-induced meningitis that left him with a renewed urge to write. He also needed money. He had drafted and redrafted the bulk of his book, and applied for a Guggenheim as well as a PEN Center West Writers with AIDS award, which his work went on to win after his death. He had begun a novel and was teaching at the University of Arizona. He had grown closer to several of his friends as well, including a man named Ted Hand, a young father and artist still figuring out his way in the world, who shared Robin's love for the desert. Robin had made a trip to Los Angeles to track down some of the gay male porn stars of the previous generation, whose fates in the age of AIDS would further limn the lives of gay men amid a crisis of desire. And he aimed as well to go to a reunited Germany, to compare the freedoms of gay male sexuality in the age of the Iron Curtain with the strictures imposed on gay men in a reunited Germany dealing with AIDS. He would also try to search out the man who had infected him.

He had also told me that he was growing restless in Tucson and that maybe it would soon become time to go back to New York, if he could do it healthfully. He probably wouldn't want to live in the city, he said — maybe someplace nearby. I would find out later that he had only a hundred T cells (the average healthy person has close to one thousand). I resolved to myself that when he was ready, I would help him find a little house, a Northeast version of his adobe dwelling.

After mailing off his manuscript, Robin left with Ted Hand for a week of hiking in the Tonto National Forest, east of Phoenix, a starkly beautiful landscape of cactus, arroyos, and steep ravines. On a foray away from their campsite that Saturday, evening was coming quickly as Ted and Robin hurried to make it home before dark. Robin decided to take a shortcut, down a severe incline.

Robin lost his footing and slid down the ravine. He came to rest some twenty feet from the top, on a ledge, his left leg tangled beneath him. Ted followed him down, with difficulty. It was clear that Robin's leg was broken and that he couldn't move. Night was falling fast, as Robin knew it would. "The further south one goes," he had written, "the more abrupt the transition from daylight to darkness." Ted could not leave to get help and be sure that he could find Robin again in the dark. They would have to spend the night braced against the side of the ravine.

Ted built a fire to cut the intense desert cold. Robin was cogent, and they talked as night fell on them. Robin said they should have made a propitiation to Hermes before they left Tucson; that was what caused this, he told Ted. As the two of them drowsed through the night, Robin's pain grew worse. He kept talking to Ted, but delirium pulled at him. Once he called Ted by another name.

When dawn finally came, Ted positioned Robin as comfortably as he could and scrambled upward onto the plane of the desert. He turned and took a photograph of Robin before he rushed off to seek help. Soon he ran into some other hikers who had a cell phone. A helicopter circled in to pick up Ted and take him to where Robin lay. But when they arrived at the place where Ted had left him, Robin was not there. He had slid farther, dropping another sixty feet to the bottom of the ravine, where he had died on impact.

Usually when someone dies, the first memory of him that fades is his voice, his timbre fraying into the atmosphere. Robin's voice stays with me, more sturdy than a signal from a satellite. It remains full-bodied.

Robin Hardy left behind more than half of the manuscript he intended to write, including the first chapter and the last three, which make up the thematic bulk of his book and complete its basic arc. We know his starting place, and we also know his destination: his vision of what we have lost to AIDS and what we might regain. My job was to let his voice guide me to complete the trail he opened.

Robin wrote at the nadir of hope for AIDS. He had seen the advent of protease inhibitors, but he did not live to witness the way the new "drug cocktail" gave people with HIV their first sustained shot at survival. Certain chapters, particularly one on AIDS medicine, which Robin had titled "The Machinery of Death," needed revamping in light of current situations and controversies. Yet I was struck by how his basic points have only been reaffirmed by the continuing course of AIDS and how easy it was to advance his arguments into the present. Gay men who want to take charge of their health care now face medical, financial, and psychological issues that are more complicated than ever. And they are doing so in the dark, within a society that now has an excuse to believe that AIDS is over.

While the tone of the battle against AIDS has changed, the basic issues that Robin addresses have, if anything, grown even more aggravated. Huge inequities continue between those people who can afford the drugs and those who can't. The outside world is washing the hands it never really soiled in the first place, slapping scientists on the back even as it averts its eyes from HIV's ravages past and

present. Gay men know better — that the drugs work for some, but
that others are still slated to die.

Gay men have been fighting AIDS longer than America fought
the Vietnam War. They are tired, angry, traumatized, and confused.
The diminution of gay men in the AIDS epidemic persists, even as
their role changes and the epidemic reshapes itself demographi-
cally. Their true sexual desires continue to be thwarted, dangerously, by the specter of AIDS. And even though AIDS has brought
them together, given them new national and community institutions, and shown how capably they provide their brothers with critical care, they remain distracted from the broad possibilities that the
Stonewall revolution offered: the chance to build a new community of affections. In his first chapter, Robin addresses his readers
with this provocative statement: "AIDS is over. Gay men lost." In
the most recent phase of the war against HIV disease, that pro-
nouncement takes on new levels of meaning.

The crisis of desire continues to rage. Gay men have less idea
than ever how their sexuality might sustain them. Writers Gabriel
Rotello and Michelangelo Signorile have stirred angry debate about
the construction of gay male sexuality — basically asking whether
gay men should define monogamous, private relationships as both
an epidemiological and social goal. Does gay male "multipart-
nerism" remain a major contributing factor to the surge of the epidemic, as Rotello would have it, or can sexual adventuring be made
safe enough from HIV that it becomes a core value for gay men
celebrating their bodies and their sexuality? What if it is both?
Robin had long been conducting his own internal conversation on
these issues. As I've augmented what Robin has written in this regard, I have tried to speak from his point of view even as I value the
concerns his adversaries have raised. I remain persuaded that gay
men must create for themselves a community fully animated by all
the possibilities of desire.

Several chapters Robin planned to write cannot be reclaimed.

Nobody can go to Berlin to relive Robin's years there and find the man who may have infected him in 1983. Nor can anyone trace the men and meanings of 1980s gay pornography the way Robin would have. On certain subjects he simply didn't leave behind enough information for me to reconstruct his argument. The specifics of his complaint against American death and funerary practices are lost. So is much of his bill of particulars against AIDS-related films, theater, and literature — nearly all of which Robin believed were just as sentimental, marginalizing, and politically emasculating as the ubiquitous red ribbon that signifies that most modestly defined concern, "AIDS awareness."

Robin's files contain more than one hundred pages of typed notes that I have ordered, assembled, and elaborated upon in the book's second chapter, "The Crisis of Desire." The chapter starts with Robin's account of his experience in Berlin in 1983 and lays out the specifics of the crisis faced by gay men whose lives have been shortened, warped, and limited by the virus.

Robin wanted to call this book "The Landscape of Death." While the term is a vital part of the book's vocabulary, it is a bummer of a title. Another possible title, "The Enemy of Love," seemed to feature the virus too much and not enough the lives of the gay men affected by it. Ultimately, the best title for the book seemed the one Robin had thought of first, back when he was drafting his book proposal. *The Crisis of Desire* harks back to a seminal book by Frank Browning that sought to define gay male society, *The Culture of Desire*. The title also does more justice to the urgency of Robin's philosophical agenda and suggests its possibilities — that even in the enduring earthquake of AIDS we can reclaim and rebuild the landscape we have lost.

Some people will like what they read here. Others will find their sacred cows sacrificed or ignored, dismissed to other pastures without a word. *The Crisis of Desire* is not a comprehensive account of gay men and AIDS, nor is it a detailed manifesto for political and social change. With all its omissions, obsessions, brilliance, and provocation, it is one man's vision. Robin's book is among the first AIDS testimonies written by an HIV-positive gay man. I hope myriad gay men — seropositive or seronegative — will finally hear a version of their own voices resonate.

Robin Hardy may have fallen to his death, but he also did die of AIDS. What led him to the edge of that ravine was, for want of a better word, fate — fate being some mechanism of luck and a choice, some combination of shoe leather and pressure on the sand beneath it. Surely AIDS is a part of that fate. AIDS caused Robin to retreat to Tucson; AIDS made Robin mail that package to his editor that particular afternoon. AIDS made Robin hurry.

Had he followed in the manner of several hundred thousand North American men, women, and children before him, Robin might well have died the old-fashioned way, the way people with AIDS are supposed to — in a bed, wasting away sadly but expectably. With that sort of death we would have possessed a protocol of grief and a received set of meanings to apply to his departure. But Robin, dying as headlong as he lived, trumped those meanings. He has become, more than he was in life, both the author and subject of his work. He died *with* AIDS. His death summons his theme: the premature loss of gay men. Yet it reaches beyond that theme as well, to the kind of experience of human and natural history that Robin felt in the Gila Wilderness and writes about in his first chapter. Because it fits no pattern, our grief for him twists back on itself to be more complicated, less categorical and reflexive. Robin would like that, I believe, because in his life and work he asked us to rethink and refeel the transactions we have with life and death — to plunge past the protocols to the hard truths.

At Robin's New York memorial service, his sister Eloise Hardy showed me the photograph Ted had taken that Sunday morning when he clambered out of the ravine and turned, for whatever documentary or primal reason, to record Robin. Confronted with the tangle of jeans, the blue bright against the brown blur of desert, his face and body obscured by the brush, and knowing what would happen only minutes later, I had to look away. It is never pretty to romanticize death; Robin decries that in these very pages. But it is worse to turn aside from it, for to deny the brutal truth of the body in death is to deny its life as well. I give Robin's death its due. I believe — I think Robin would have me believe — that as he slid down that ravine his body felt not just pain and terror but some kind of exhilaration. Robin is not falling but flying. That is life and death in one moment. As I hand over his words to his readers, I hope we can all continue Robin's work: to take on the mortal risk of loving.

[1]

The Enemy of Love

AIDS AND ITS MYTHS

HIV TICKS, A SILENT time bomb in my veins.

My blood and semen are poison to my species. My body has been commandeered by a lethal alien, the genetic crumbs of creation, possessed of the improbable power to forge a molecular lock on certain cells of the human immune system. It is programmed with only the most basic imperative of existence: propagate; replicate; reproduce.

The genes of the human immunodeficiency virus have engineered a takeover of the factory that is my body. The virus is retooling me to its own use — making copies and reassembling itself. These stray bits of DNA become me, are me, and I am HIV, as much literally in the genetic codes of my cells as in the figurative way that HIV will define me for the rest of my life. The work of the virus is to kill me, just as it has killed over three hundred thousand gay men like me in North America, along with several million heterosexuals throughout the world.

Since 1981, when AIDS first loomed over us, we have not cured AIDS or saved those lives — not because we do not know how, but because we lack the social will. Instead, we have been captive to a

series of exquisitely pervasive illusions that keep us from caring too
deeply or committing ourselves too absolutely to the defeat of the
virus. We believe that behavioral changes alone will control the
epidemic. We conclude we are helpless and ignorant in the face
of a diabolical virus that outwits our greatest brains, our most advanced technologies. We make AIDS an affliction of the Other,
those gay or poor or drug-using people who are not us and are
thus somehow not as human as we are, who are thus objects of sympathy, sentiment, and separation. When we hear news of drugs that
seem to be working on HIV, we fold AIDS away like the memory
of Vietnam — even as the Centers for Disease Control and Prevention announce that 31,153 new cases of AIDS were reported in
America in 1997. We wear red ribbons at the Emmys. We decline to
face death; we skirt sexuality, make sex the enemy. Like almost
every other human society, ours mistakes the forces of culture and
history for the mandates of nature. We deny that, in certain ways,
the existence of AIDS works for us.

AIDS today is business, charity, cautionary tale, old news —
certainly no longer a crisis. From social support to drug development to viatical settlements for life insurance, an industry has
sprung from the suffering of victims. Scientists and doctors stake
careers on their research. Government largesse endows millions
to laboratories. Philanthropists and moguls bestow their names on
sex-education and HIV-research institutes. From the efficient official business of AIDS arises the marginalization of people afflicted
or traumatized by the disease — and the denial of the essence of
gay men themselves. Because of our systems of denial, a singular
and important generation of gay American men has been allowed
to die.

Only the virus endures, no longer a crisis, but lingering like
Muzak in the background at ghetto parades, in communities narco-
tized with red ribbons, busy with sentimental notions and symbolic

observations that conceal the evidence of the continuing slaughter we rush to leave behind. They sing: AIDS is over. Gay men lost.

So powerful are the many myths surrounding HIV that, if it had not burst from the rain forest to do its deadly work, you wonder if, like God, our culture would not have had to invent it. Critics have already noted that AIDS, as British activist Simon Watney wrote in his book *Practices of Freedom*, "is invariably made to carry a supplement of fantasy which both precedes and exceeds any actual medical issues . . . ideological manoeuvres which unconsciously 'make sense' of this accidental triangulation of disease, sexuality and homophobia."

In the most elemental recesses of human consciousness, the human immunodeficiency virus represents an intrusion of chaos, the boundaries of an orderly world breached by something mysterious and unknown. To protect ourselves from that void, we create stories. Myth is the autopilot of consciousness; we plunder cultural myths for refuge, sort through symbols, stereotypes, parables, and contradictions, until we assemble a narrative that somehow makes sense to us and keeps our fears at bay.

Unfortunately, the possibilities that myths provide are limited. They give simple if potent answers for complicated and problematic phenomena. Myths are not about what is. They are about what people want.

For some, HIV is damnation from a god of many rules, the god that informs you that if you like your body too much and celebrate its sexual pleasures, or somehow don't love yourself enough, you will be punished with a disease that will kill you. Others believe that the CIA field-tested a terrific new biological warfare agent in the ventilation systems of gay bathhouses in New York, exposing a disposable population to a germ it could use to kill enemies. (It's not that far-fetched a theory: the U.S. Army Special Operations

Division admits its operatives tossed supposedly harmless gas-filled bulbs onto the tracks of the Manhattan A train, as a test. More than thirty years after the experiment, the identity of that gas is still classified information.) An astonishing proportion of people of color are persuaded that the government has used HIV the way it is claimed it used crack, to keep a minority population in place — and isn't it politically convenient that HIV has a predilection for young black and Latino men and women?

And for yet other people, AIDS is a solution for whatever else has been troubling their lives. Like the prospect of hanging, it can focus their attentions on living in a way that their uninfected routines could not. HIV can make a man swear off anything the world tells him is a vice, from drinking to sexuality. It can also allow him license to drown his fate in drugs or practice infective sex. It can corroborate the inner hatred the outer world bequeaths him. HIV can excuse him from facing the issues of growing old and remaining committed to the world. Especially for gay men, from whom AIDS stole the ones who would have shown them how to age, there is the James Dean–Marilyn Monroe model, the god and goddess of eternal youth and beauty, who live fast and die young. Death will finally solve the problem or end the appetite.

These myths about the cause and meaning of AIDS, together with a dozen more propounded by those who suffer from HIV and those who witness that suffering, are understandable, human, and pernicious. The myths exist for all of us. For a few who can keep a clear head at least some of the time, AIDS remains only a tiny bundle of proteins, an entity caught between existence and the abyss, unleashed among humans by demographic movements, its spread precisely mapped by the principles of epidemiology.

Certain passages in literature written in the 1970s seem to prophesy the coming plague, as if the trauma rippled back through time. In his novel *Cities of the Red Night*, William Burroughs portrays his eponyms with images of the Castro or Christopher Street at their most hedonistic, and the imagined civilization is destroyed when "a virus crept through the barriers of time," causing people to orgasm to death. Burroughs wrote that novel, published the same month as the first reported case of "gay cancer" in 1981, while HIV was spreading, silent and unknown, among gay men.

In all his work, Burroughs's vision of the orgasm has always been partly curse and partly a means of transcendence. But a virus that creeps through the barriers of time is a perfect metaphor for the potency of our cultural myths. They seep into us without our knowing it. They gain even greater power in times of duress — as when a generation is in the process of throwing aside a system of sexual control whose thick roots germinated in a nomadic tribe in the Sinai four millennia ago.

In AIDS, the ancient myth of the homosexual as criminal, and the twentieth-century psychiatric myth of the homosexual as mentally ill, were reinvigorated by a new bond between the homosexual and a deadly, contagious plague. With their implications of quarantine, confinement, behavior modification, recidivism, and containment — not to mention the biters, spitters, monsters, and homicidal dentists in our midst who are accused of spreading the virus wantonly — the myths of homosexual illness and homosexual criminality were instantly entwined like strands of RNA. This time, the connection that spawned the myths was not merely prejudicial, metaphysical, or even theoretical. It was scientifically verifiable. It was very, very real.

I have never been particularly enthralled by illness's myths and metaphors, I think because I grew up the second of five children, among whom two brothers, one older, one younger, were born with cystic fibrosis. It is an incurable illness of the exocrine glands, genetically inherited. The organs fill with mucus, preventing digestion, causing malnutrition. The lungs become the perfect breeding culture for common bacteria, harmless to most of us, but killers for people with CF.

The sources of my older brother Christopher's anger were many — at least as much the doctors' pessimism as the unfair genetic hand he'd been dealt. I think his fury was unwillingly but inevitably directed at me from the moment I was born. I arrived close by his second birthday, a baby plump, pink, and healthy. Somewhere deep within his sickly body, he already knew that someday I would win the ultimate contest of our sibling rivalry by decree of nature: I would outlive him.

We were also intimately brothers, though, our boys' lives the sum of our mutual growing up. From toddler to teenager, the time when a couple of years make a big difference in the sum of life's experiences and a child's command of his environment, my older brother led me into the world beyond the nuclear family, brazenly, as only a child can. He was my earliest teacher and mentor. Each night, in beds in the same room, as sleep came down we spoke our deepest confidences to each other, while beyond the window a northern prairie twilight seeped away to our comic-book dreams of superheroes and space travel.

Life expectancy for people with CF is still only about twenty-two years. When Chris was diagnosed, it was a children's disease, and he was expected to die before adolescence. In 1984, at his thirty-fourth birthday, he was one of the few surviving CF adults in the world. We celebrated, and after dinner went to a movie. We arrived late at the theater, and I began to rush across the parking lot. He called out to me and asked me to slow down. He had always been a vehemently independent man, shouldering past his own maladies, and never before had he asked for a concession to his illness. He'd had a chest infection since earlier in the year, and this time he couldn't shake it, even after two bouts of antibiotic drips in the hospital. I fell into step beside him. He coughed, and horked into a Kleenex, took it away from his mouth, glanced at it, then showed it to me. In the little glistening glob of mucus was a tiny dark red speck.

"Blood?" I asked, already disturbed and perplexed.

He shook his head. "Tissue."

I took a second look at the Kleenex before I understood what Christopher meant. Not paper tissue — human tissue. He was coughing up bits of his disintegrating lungs.

Chris's death a few months later marked the beginning of the time when AIDS became a visceral part of my life. Although neither of us had the slightest clue that moment in the parking lot observing a speck of lung, Chris has led the way once more across an invisible frontier.

Well before Christopher took his last breaths, gay men in North America had stumbled into the war zone that is AIDS. With the death of Rock Hudson in 1985, the rest of America got into the act, the fact of celebrity making the devastation as real as television. Americans would begin to observe AIDS the way residents of Washington, D.C., had packed their picnics and boarded their carriages to see the first Civil War battle, the first battle of Bull Run, in 1861; they would sit on the ridge, out of the line of fire, spectators stirred into sentiment. For gay men, the reality of AIDS means surviving in the trenches. It remains immediate, unpredictable, and cruel. AIDS began as if with a shot from a sniper, when someone we knew well got really sick. It continues now with the inhaled breath, held, as we wait for the sound of gunfire.

After Chris's death, in rapid succession my friends began to die from AIDS: Don Bell, an old roommate, mysteriously ill and out of sight; several months later, Steven Flint, a boyfriend from years earlier. AIDS roamed at the periphery of my life, tightening slowly around a circle of friends, who began to disappear like houseguests in a murder mystery. Timo. Arty. Cliff. Tim. Jay. Ron.

Unlike my brother, my friends and I had always been healthy and able. Unlike most of my friends, I had understood terminal illness to be part of my life from my earliest memory. Chris's experience became my own guide. I saw diagnosed friends go through everything from credit-card binges to religious conversions and New Age panaceas. I recalled similar fatalistic, reckless days — innumerable auto collisions — when Chris was nineteen and twenty years old: while his high school friends went on to college or marriage, he presumed a life expectancy of twenty-one years. My friends were living that way as they sickened, their futures truncated, their trust in time stolen.

I began to feel in irrational moments that Christopher's death sentence had passed mysteriously to me. In sleep, I began to dream I was driving at night, terrified, in a car with no headlights, Christopher riding silently in the seat beside me; I was unable to see the road ahead yet moving inexorably forward, crossed fingers as my only guide; I spoke loudly in a crowded room, where people milled about oblivious to my words, as if I had already ceased to exist; I was in the basement rec room of my family's home, and it was filled with disembodied dicks, like the dildos stacked in bins at Frederick's of Hollywood, and my mother was at the door! Not my real mother, of course, but Kali, mother, avenger, destroyer, who holds the freshly severed heads of her babies in each of her eight extended hands.

That was my own, personal, potent myth, and it seemed true. The physical body I possessed now proposed death to me. Semen, traditionally sacred in human cultures, was apparently toxic. I felt as if I had regressed, that I had lost the hard-won confidence of my gay male body. Sex began to seem bad again, as it had been before closets were abandoned. Desire disappeared, the deepest instincts of an animal turning from danger.

New York, once a city that glittered and beckoned like a factory of dreams, had become Gothic, accursed, a *Titanic* sinking down to darkness in icy black waters. It was the epicenter of a postmodern epidemic, and it was the place I had gone in the wake of my brother's death to reinvest myself as a vital gay man. I felt threatened in this oppressed and oppressive city. Christopher Street, the grand boulevard of the Stonewall generation, had become for us a Burma Road. Returning to the ardently gay places I had stridden through, I found the sidewalks and bars empty except for drug addicts, hustlers, and muggers, and a few alcoholic, stunned survivors, their desires devolved into primal reflex and longing.

One night, in the autumn of 1985, after an evening of worried talk with friends who are all now dead, I sat on a bench in the park at Abingdon Square in Greenwich Village, the city pulsating around me with sexuality and panic. For a few brief seconds I stood on the edge of that terror, and realized, irrevocably, that there was no going back. For the shallowest part of a millisecond, I thought I sensed a virus pouring through my veins like lights flashing in sequence around the edge of a marquee. Whether I liked it or not, I — and almost everyone I knew — were all embarking on a great and terrible adventure from which, regrettably, there was to be no return. In the newest frontier of the landscape of death, I was bound to my brother by fate as well as birth.

When Chris was twenty-seven — and, much to his own surprise, still alive — his closest friend, a vital, healthy man, was killed in a motorcycle accident. The fact of this man's death devastated Chris, and not just because his demise was sudden and violent. Christopher's hierarchy of expectations had been instantly shattered. Everyone else was supposed to survive to old age except him. A few years later, when all the experts told me that HIV infection automatically meant death, I recalled this example of the Reaper's caprice. I had colluded in my brother's logic; for I too had thought that I would be exempt from having to take a number and get in line to be sent to oblivion.

Yet there are limits to what cystic fibrosis could tell me about the new terrain I had crossed into. Here there were far more mythical beasts and perverse magnetic forces at work. AIDS is not a congenital disease striking children in the bloom of their innocence. It fails to induce the kind of pity granted to those who are martyred by, for instance, their genes. AIDS is sex, race, gender, class, and our shadow; it is apocalypse, a whirlwind of terror of chaos and homosexuality, righteousness and disease, pleasure and pain. It stirs fears and incites conspiracy theories; it threatens contagion; it makes us hurry to separate ourselves, to keep it as far away as an extended arm with its pointed finger.

The narratives drawn from our common myths that shaped the perceptions and progress of the epidemic may twist the individual course of HIV disease as well. And certainly, tragically, infuriatingly, those myths are responsible for the first decisions around AIDS that our society made. Among them was the resolution to write off the lives of all those already infected with HIV. Whether the CIA released it or whether the rain forest did it on its own, here was an opportunity for the opponents of homosexual emancipation to rid America of a particularly troublesome generation of gay men.

For the first four years of the epidemic, official inaction was official American policy. Ronald Reagan did not even utter the word *AIDS* until 1987. Such malign neglect was "an adaptation of Adolf Hitler's 'Final Solution,'" claims Robert Searles Walker, a noted medical writer on AIDS, in his book *AIDS Today, Tomorrow*. He adds with great understatement that "it was and remains a tragic departure from standard American policy in such matters." The enemies of gay men had found their extraconstitutional policeman, and it was in our blood.

The government disdained the study of infected cells. It prioritized vaccines and safer sex to protect the innocent, which is to say the as-yet uninfected. Our culture's shaman class — scientists, doctors, and researchers — reinforced these efforts through what, in another context, author Andrew Weil calls "medical hexing," by creating a pervasive atmosphere of pessimism. Within months of the first reports in 1981 of "gay cancer," leading scientists publicly declared that everyone affected would die. Translated into press boilerplates, the word *doomed* or *fatal* appeared in virtually every news report. Repeated often enough, this conjecture became accepted truth, although scientific data have always contradicted it. AIDS is a killer disease. It has not ever been under control. But as scientists are just now getting around to emphasizing, all sorts of people survive HIV infection asymptomatically for decades; others resist infection totally or never become virulent. The evidence for these phenomena has been whispered about for years among people with HIV, but it contradicted the prevalent myth that AIDS had to mean death. For more than a decade, the most pervasive opportunistic infection of AIDS, and one engendered by the power of the medical establishment, was despair.

Medical knowledge that might have saved thousands of lives sat on the shelves of medical libraries, unused; gay men with pneumocystis carinii pneumonia (PCP) were shunted into placebo wings of trials where men and women in white lab coats watched them slowly suffocate. Each time a new discovery or breakthrough is announced, scientists enact a ritual, hurrying to assure the public with words that are an incantation for the fulfillment of prophecy: "It will be years before this translates into treatment." Or, once the drug gets into bodies, "We don't know how long the treatment will be efficacious." Emphasizing to a person that his house may blow away tomorrow does not encourage him to inhabit his house today.

The 1993 AIDS conference in Berlin was so dispiriting — not just in terms of medical progress but in terms of tone — that the press dubbed it "AIDS's bleakest moment." In the months afterward, the death rate from AIDS in San Francisco doubled, from around two hundred to four hundred a month. In New South Wales, Australia, the rate of opportunistic infections among PWAs skyrocketed. Although it cannot be measured by steel instruments and recorded on a chart, these extra dead people appear to have just given up.

Only the power of myth could so wholly overwhelm the fruits of scientific method. Positing that once infected there was no escape, the prophecies of medical shamans became the process of wish fulfillment, effectively denying the single constant of survival: hope.

There exists in the Western world a kind of apartheid around AIDS.

The "general population," people who by definition are excluded from known "risk groups" for HIV, live in a country apart from AIDS, far across a Gazan desert on the other side of wire fences. The seropositive see them roaming, their eyes half closed, glazed by the stupor of a too-pure sun.

It is not unusual for a nation to have a population of young men about to die or already dead: sending ignorant armies to fight and kill is patriotic sport, socially endorsed and highly honored. Most wars have cheerleaders. The ones who fight and die in them may be sacrificed on the altar of human stupidity, but in life and death they are embraced, included, and mourned. Even with Vietnam, America came around to embrace its veterans and its dead. Pandemics, too, have long been matters that touched everyone. Until AIDS, infectious microbes were universally dangerous. From the black plague of the 1300s to the influenza epidemic of 1918 to polio in the 1950s, germs and viruses were egalitarian killers and cripplers; even when they arose in slums or slipped in from foreign countries, and even when they were assigned their own problematic meanings, they induced a democratic panic.

But AIDS is different. HIV is as specific as ZIP-code target marketing. The estrangement of the HIV-positive mirrors the disharmony in their bodies. They live in a parallel universe, coexisting with, but largely invisible to, what the world insists on calling by the most unkind and exclusionary name in the entire AIDS lexicon: the "general population."

Soldiers returning to America from the horrors of Vietnam found an oddly incongruous country where life went on as usual, with the killing fields of the Tet Offensive suddenly replaced by surfboards, drive-ins, and psychedelia. The trauma they had undergone was life-gouging. But when they came home at least they were ultimately safe from their enemies. People with HIV carry the enemy in their blood, but they live among people who tend to regard them as less useful than cannon fodder.

In their partitioned-off territory, the seropositive have played for time and read the signposts of their future in wasting bodies — the corpses of friends stacked like firewood — and in their own uncertain reactions to drugs that may suppress the virus for years or months or not at all. Swallowing their protease inhibitors, they continue to live under sentence of death, hopeful that their penalty may be commuted to life, but still half-expecting the axe of a slow-motion executioner. Among them the mentality of fear and scarcity has become ubiquitous, and the prospect of a future teases them. It is life in wartime, and they have become an occupied population. They have gotten so used to the siege that they barely acknowledge it anymore, enduring as they do the daily, yearly, scrounge for survival.

Which is not to say that the sunny country of noninfection hasn't also been dimmed by AIDS. The media may not give its inhabitants many consistent reports from the territory of the HIV-positive, for if nothing *new* has happened — if only another 109 new cases of AIDS are diagnosed today, if no new drug has caused its maker's stock price to soar — then no news has happened. Occasionally the press will relay to them a story of a gay man with AIDS, especially if he is somehow exceptional or affects their livelihood in some way. Often the media will observe how the deaths of gay men touch the general population. The *New York Times* ran a long home-living piece on what to do when the interior decorator dies halfway through the job. Society women bemoan the loss of their favorite hairdresser. The 1990s, we were told, would become the "decade of the woman designer" (because many gay men were redlined by garment-industry investors, or dead); we all hear of the new lesbian visibility in the queer movement (not only because lesbians are competent and confident but because an entire generation of gay male leadership is dead). We see movies and television shows about gay men with AIDS, but almost without exception the presumption by producers and programmers is that human sympathy thrives only close to home. And thus the camera will focus on Aidan Quinn's parents; Richard Thomas's lover's mother; Tom Hanks's heterosexual lawyer; Ryan White's mother; young, straight Alison Gertz and her family. Gay men, indeed everyone with HIV in his or her bloodstream, gets shunted to the side in the popular communication of their own tragedy.

In the film *Philadelphia*'s family scenes, heterosexual kinfolk were consumed by squalling babies and small children, a profusion of life occurring while the sun poured through suburban windows. The movie's gay men lived in cinematic shadows as well as the shadow of death. This contrast is the invention of moviemakers heroizing heterosexual concern for AIDS victims in the family. But for people living with AIDS in their lives or their bodies, those constant shadows have their own truth that has nothing to do with Hollywood. For a survivor, the strangest thing when someone dies with AIDS is that the rest of the world goes on in all its picayune detail. He is thrust into a weird solipsism while everyone else plunges forward like a relentless subway train, full of appetency. Social scientists have invented a name — Multiple Bereavement Syndrome, or MBS — to describe the disordered psychologies of gay men who have watched dozens of friends and lovers die, their grief compounded by the world's hearty heedlessness.

With the demise of AIDS activism in the early 1990s, the natural allies of the infected — seronegative gay men — fell victim to this relentless deprivation of hope. Their despair has often since been translated into sexual negativism, self-preservation at the expense of empathy for their infected gay brothers, increased sexual risk, and the most banal forms of sentimentality, as when a prominent New York jeweler began selling platinum red ribbons set with garnets — permitting a link between the gesture's monetary value and an individual's measure of ostentatious, useless concern.

At a time when the gay community embraced the issue of the right of homosexuals to serve in the military, with a palpable sense of relief at moving the political agenda away from disease and onto patriotic territory, the position of gay men with HIV in the gay communities became ironically analogous to the myth of the spurned and shunned veteran. In a decade after the Stonewall riots, gay men had rather successfully begun the task of redefining civil sexuality and the bonds all humans might be free to create. Now, ignoring the profound, revolutionary accomplishments of the post-Stonewall generation, a new array of activists lobbies and litigates for the right to marry. One of their main arguments claims that marriage would tame gay men, make them settle down, and thus reduce the spread of AIDS. That contention is not geared to the gay community; it is put forth as a crowd pleaser for heterosexual media and legislators fearful of AIDS and ignorant about how it works. Such rhetoric effectively, wrongly, and cruelly disenfranchises, desexualizes, and demonizes every single gay man with AIDS.

With this kind of dismissal in the body of the gay community and from a general population afraid of AIDS and bored by it, how could gay men with HIV feel anything but despair and estrangement? Certain drugs may diminish the level of virus in our bodies, but there remains no end to our exile.

"Bongo is dead. Ter Braak. DuPerron, Marsman, all are dead. Pos, and van den Bergh and many others are in concentration camps . . ." Although *concentration camp* is used instead of *hospital*, the words sound chillingly familiar. They were written in the diary of a Dutch Jewess named Etty Hillesum, who was killed at Auschwitz on

November 30, 1943. Her diaries were published under the title *An Interrupted Life* and describe Amsterdam under the Nazi occupation. "So many of our most promising, vigorous young men are dying day and night. I don't know how to take it."

In this terrifying era of lost friends, Etty Hillesum, together with my brother Chris, has become a constant companion. I recognized her immediately, not as an alter ego, but as someone who would certainly have been a friend. She wrote about her lovers, and sex was a way for her to express an almost overwhelming love for existence. "I have broken my body like bread and shared it out among men. And why not, they were hungry and had gone without for so long," she wrote in one of her last letters. And yet her dream is a familiar, intimate one: "A man for life, and build something together with . . ."

As many people have found they must in the AIDS crisis, Etty Hillesum was forced to "look suffering directly in the face" without fear. While she affirmed, "I want to live to see the future," she was also under no illusions when she speculated about the enemy's intentions: "Of course, it is our complete destruction they want!" And like many gay men who dealt with AIDS, Etty Hillesum wrestled with an essential question: To what degree acceptance? to what degree protest?

In the age of AIDS, gay men are well aware of the old myths about homosexuality and how they operated to maintain a certain moral status quo. Their adult lives as openly gay men had been lived on the other side of a chasm that separates their daily reality from narratives of homosexuality subscribed to by that chimera, the "general population," in its many semantic guises. When "gay cancer" officially became "Gay Related Immune Deficiency" — that first, wildly inaccurate term that the medical establishment applied to the set of symptoms it beheld — such labels seemed suspiciously like new versions of the sick homosexual; when stigma resulted in persecution, once again the homosexual was rendered criminal.

To meet this new and deadly adversary, and to circumvent the inane social response to it, gay men came together to employ the same tactics they had acquired in a decade of building gay communities, adding another layer of institutions to focus on health care: Gay Men's Health Crisis, AIDS Project Los Angeles, Project Angel Food, and hundreds of others. When no treatments were forthcoming, gay men pored through the pharmaceutical armamentariums of foreign countries and alternative healing systems. They set up smuggling networks to expand the availability of treatments, bringing in hopeful drugs like Compound Q in from Asia. They began buyers' clubs in defiance of federal regulation. They challenged the hegemony of scientists and doctors over research priorities and medical decisions. Man by man, they turned into experts, juggling drug acronyms with ease, jumping ahead of their doctors' knowledge. If gay men were forced to be patients, they were determined not to abdicate control over their physical bodies. This is a central tenet of AIDS activism. It is a profound gift given by people with AIDS to all people with illness — the notion that they have a right to be masters of their own health care.

A deeply held principle of the baby-boom generation was at work: that the personal is political. Reduced by feminists into its most succinct and popular form was the belief that our bodies belong to ourselves. No other idea has been so powerful in the last half of the twentieth century. It began with the civil rights movement, when African Americans refused to be controlled because of the color of their skin, and it underlay the resistance of young men to fighting an immoral war in Vietnam. It encouraged a generation to use "mind-expanding" psychotropic drugs and indulge in free love. As feminists insisted on a woman's right to control her reproductive decision-making, gay liberationists extended the concept of personal autonomy to sexual decision-making, and they began to question the entire multimillennial edifice of desire, pleasure, and the body.

Rooting political action in the experience of the body determined the course of AIDS activism. Suddenly, health and wellness decision-making became political. Finally, when dying men began to commit suicide in the most covert and barren of circumstances, the principle of autonomy over the body was extended to its last frontier: the right to self-termination, or euthanasia.

At the beginning of the crisis, gay men insisted on safer-sex advocacy to redefine sexual practices in an epidemic. They would work hard to take command of the epidemic, even as they struggled with insufficient knowledge about what sexual safety should entail, as well as fierce opposition from a sex-phobic government. Moreover, gay men with AIDS quickly realized that control over the myth-infused language of their altered identity was crucial. They declined the rubric of "victim" in favor of "person living with AIDS" — the invention of the PWA. Coming out as a PWA, like coming out as homosexual, challenged yet another manifestation of the pariah. The AIDS crisis made twelve years of post-Stonewall liberation seem like a dress rehearsal for the main event.

Control over one's body was part of a social contract that emerged after World War II. The other side of the equation was a greater individual moral duty: to act to stop evil. "Following orders" no longer vindicated someone who had committed crimes against humanity, a principle established at Nuremberg, and reinforced for the baby-boom generation by the Eichmann trial in 1961. Evil was all the more terrifying for its banality: Hannah Arendt gave us a vision of the good family man as the scion of darkness — the bureaucrat, *Homo institutus*, calmly stamping requisitions for bars of soap made from human fat, and for electrical conductors insulated with Jewish hair.

In the face of the utter disregard of the "general population" for their plight, many gay men were astonished and disappointed. A lot of privileged white men were shocked to realize they were cheap meat. They had expected the great American daddy to assist them in combating a virus that did evil things. But here the postwar social contract failed and the Western world denied its moral duty. While certain scientists, doctors, politicians, and mothers might care enough to act, they were subsumed by a larger establishment that just didn't care very much. It was never possible for our culture to extend an arm of help to the drowning man. No matter what people with AIDS did to try to crush the virus among them, the myths around AIDS would prevail. The result would mean that gay men took their place in the tale as the perpetrator homosexual, the criminal, the diseased pariah, and — standing in for a generation's conflict about the body — a scapegoat.

In October 1984, I drove to an Ottawa hospital to see my brother during one of his routine stays. Indian summer was over, the Rideau River was shrouded in an icy fog, the gaunt black branches of trees glistened in the streetlights, leaf-naked and wet. When I saw the backlit blue sign with its big white *H* glowing in the twilight, I felt, almost as if the air had slapped me, a thud of trepidation that increased when I turned into the long landscaped drive, and the modern hospital loomed across an empty lake of parking spaces. It hit me all at once, the realness, the sadness, the horror of Chris's situation: that he was here in the hospital on the edge of town. At my brother's bedside, I took one look at him and knew instantly that this was it. He was going to die, and soon.

Dying is not operatic passion; it's utterly mundane. The dying are concerned about picky, little things that have become monumentally important: a glass of water in a certain spot on the bedside table; keeping all but the closest friends at bay. I tried to talk to Chris about dying, but it was the one thing he could not do. He was not always one to communicate. His doctors, like the ones who'd predicted his death in childhood, now told us he would be an invalid for eight months to a year before his lungs gave out completely. It was suggested that the family explore options for round-the-clock home care.

That arrangement never interested Chris. After he made his goodbyes, he died within a week, slipping through an open door in dreams, peacefully, in sleep, at sunrise.

To have cystic fibrosis, a person must inherit two recessive genes, one from each parent. The genes can be passed down in families for generations before they come together in one marriage among twenty; the result of those copulations is a brood in which two out of four children are carriers, each with one copy of the gene, and where one is sick and one completely "normal."

The recessive gene is found mainly among Caucasians and has mutated twice: forty thousand years ago in the Pyrenees; and twenty thousand years ago in Persia or the Balkans. From both directions, the mutation spread into northern Europe. Evolutionary scientists were baffled that such a disadvantageous gene had not been filtered from the pool long ago. Only recently have they realized that the two children who each inherit one gene have a kind of "half CF": the slight changes in the digestive tract confer a certain immunity to cholera, epidemics of which have swept across Europe in waves throughout historic times. CF carriers survived in greater numbers. They carried the gene forward.

What my family had always viewed as a curse actually distributed an evolutionary advantage through kinship lines, and this was Christopher's heritage: he was a chromosomal scapegoat for the larger tribe. Nature sacrifices a life here and there along an ancestral chain in order to strengthen the bodies of many others.

People like to find redemption in this rebuke to human individuality. Redemption, after all, is the fruit of Christian faith, and in that tradition the scapegoat is wedded to the image of the Crucifixion, when the Nazarene took on the sins of the world, that the faithful might be saved for an otherworldly life: the Redeeming Victim.

This has also suited the mythic AIDS narrative: a scapegoat to expiate everyone's sexual adventures — not only in the old days before HIV, but including all the unsafe and promiscuous moments among people today. Those infected with HIV would pay pleasure's price for everyone. They would tell cautionary tales. That general population could relieve itself by dumping every guilty desire on the sickbeds of dying homosexuals.

AIDS is the source of so much suffering that it has no silver lining, despite the protestations of New Age bunnies that "AIDS is the best thing that ever happened to me!" If there is redemption in living with HIV, it is only in determining that something good can be constructed in the midst of great evil, and it can only be personal.

In an earlier tradition, the scapegoat was not the sacrifice. It was the goat that escaped into the desert — scourged and derided perhaps, abandoned by the people unto a devil named Azazel. But nevertheless alive, and free.

Il s'agit bien d'un virus qui se colle aux gens par l'acte sexuel. A virus passes among men through sex. These words were written in 1976 by Alex Barbier, a French painter, in a book called *Lycaön*, a graphic novel for which Barbier created both the illustrations and the text. Lycaon was a king of Arcadia in pre-Hellenic times. He and his fifty-two sons were turned into wild beasts when they refused to worship Zeus and instead served him human flesh at a banquet. In Ovid's *Metamorphoses*, the story is linked to Deucalion, the Moses of the Greek version of the Flood, which was caused by Zeus as punishment for King Lycaon's iniquity. (The myth retells, in symbolic terms, the story of the arrival of northern invaders with a patriarchal religion who replaced the earlier matrifocal civilizations of the eastern Mediterranean. The story of Lycaon and his sons is the origin of the modern wolf-man myth.)

Barbier transplants this ancient Greek tale to a modern world of brilliantly sunlit beaches and moonlight streaming into crumbling hotel rooms, where the narrator and his lover flee across empty landscapes, always pursued by a strange malevolence known only as a disembodied voice emitted from paper-towel dispensers in sterile, white-tiled public restrooms.

To Barbier, the virus is a metaphor for transformation: men infected with it metamorphose into Lycaons, feral wolf-dogs who tear to bloody pieces those who are merely human. In human form, the Lycaons recognize each other, infiltrate everywhere; their status is criminal. They are pursued by enemies to their ultimate deaths.

Barbier transformed the myth of Lycaon by a shift in perspective. He presented the story from the losers' point of view. The fugitive protagonists find a brief respite from their pursuit on a sun-blind beach by a blue ocean. The narrator says, "I never felt so cool. But it didn't really change my point of view." In the doomed couple's portrait is the union of renegade and outsider, homosexual and criminal, homosexual and disease, homosexual and desire — finding an apotheosis not in the summation of the content of a life, but in the substance of a single moment.

Later in the story the flood comes, water rising in the street of an abandoned city while the protagonists make love in a fleabag hotel room, awaiting death while other Lycaons stand guard, like Anubis, in the street below. Barbier suggests that life must also be lived with the affirmation of erotic love, no matter the consequence, without regard for who in the next instant will capture you and carry you away. But this story of the Lycaons is haunted too by a quality of doom similar to William Burroughs's: the duality of sex and death — postcoital *tristesse*, the sadness after ecstasy, *la petite mort*. Barbier wrote:

> You cannot mistake . . . the special sun that shines on this country we know well and find everywhere. . . . It is the landscape of death. . . . This landscape is so rich with life that nothing can stop it, it exists everywhere, goes through every face. It means: we are going to die.

This affirmation in the face of the inevitable might be the same for all of us — not that someday we will all be dead, which is obvious, but that the prospect of death gives meaning to life. One can succumb to death anytime and anyplace. By implication, choosing to live is a harder decision. It is especially difficult when death not just lingers but looms, when it is not just a persistent specter but a relentless and isolating reality, ready to pounce when some life-reviving drug gives way, as someday — sooner, later — all drugs will.

Here is a myth we can use. Barbier's rewriting of an ancient tale also calls us to construct new narratives from the old ones — not simply to accept what was chosen for others thousands of years ago. Although death may be the end result of many, even most, HIV infections, death is the fact of everyone's life. The difference is in the minutes, days, and years that stretch between now and that moment; the raw stuff of affirmation is time.

"I want to be sent to every one of the camps that lie scattered all over Europe, I want to be at every front, I don't ever want to be what they call 'safe,'" wrote Etty Hillesum, who refused the urging of friends to go into hiding. "I want to understand what is happening and share my knowledge with as many as I can possibly reach."

Etty Hillesum went to Westerbork, the camp from which Dutch Jews were transported east. "Let me be the thinking heart of these barracks," she wrote from there in a letter to a friend in Amsterdam. "That is what I want to be . . . the thinking heart of a whole concentration camp."

There is a sharp distinction between what J. G. Gaarlante in the introduction to Hillesum's diaries calls her "radical altruism" and the kind of Pollyanna pleasantries expressed by such contemporary, unconsidered pabulum as the encouragement to "make friends with your disease." Finding reasons to be reassured by the abject suffering of large numbers of people is acquiescence to prepackaged sentimentality. Etty Hillesum knew what gay men learned so profoundly at Hard Knocks High. After a night spent watching a long line of cattle cars crammed with deportees bound east to death camps, she saw Allied aircraft bomb a nearby town and wrote, completely rhetorically, "So why shouldn't it be possible for the railway line to be hit too, and for the train to be stopped from leaving?"

Mortal crisis shocks some people from the placid life, the routines and co-optations of their surroundings. At least, after various detours through anger or self-pity, it offers a chance for some renewal, however brief. The transformations around HIV that I have witnessed were amazing but never surprising to me. Friends moved through the stages of AIDS, one by one falling below borderline T-cell counts that delineated the possibilities for various "clinical events": the beginning of antiviral therapy, the first opportunistic illness, the start of wasting, the last flickers of eyesight. In each and every stage until the last, they adamantly claimed that the syndrome stopped there, that the latest strategy would stop progression. Shortly they adapted completely to whatever new reality presented itself: quivering limbs, a rotting brain, or a leopard's tithe of purple spots. In every stage they hugged life like a lover.

When the doctors opened up my brother's corpse for the autopsy they found that his pancreas was destroyed, as were most of his liver and kidneys, and the greater part of his lungs. His heart had grown to twice its normal size to pump sufficient oxygen to the distal regions of his body. The doctors were astonished. Given how little functioned, they wondered not that Chris had died, but at how long he had been alive.

From that first step in the parking lot when Chris coughed up a piece of his lung, I found myself deep in foreign territory that everyone must someday travel. The cataracts that I possessed, as many young and lively people do, were plucked away, the opaque walls that protect us, most of the time, from the very real proximity of individual extinction.

Although I live with it daily, I have never believed that I must die of AIDS. I believe only that I have been told so. The most difficult thing for people living with HIV to convey to the uninfected is that we feel our futures to be open-ended, not foreclosed — no more so than anyone else's. AIDS cannot be redemption: it's too big, too awful, the way it mocks us and sucks our blood. There are no silver linings, only the choices we make in how to shape our lives to each vital new circumstance. Redemption happens every day when our eyes open to the morning sun.

We who are living with HIV are rendered naked on the way to a destination all of us walk to. The landscape of death is the territory of all lives. In that terrain, life is full of murmuring and changing, with the babble of voice, color, size, and shape, the profusion and division of DNA, the body's molecules quivering in a warm zone at 98.6, and shot with electricity. Life is always lived with the threat of imminent death: the Reaper is at our shoulder, the tip of his scythe hovering barely in our peripheral vision.

Some days we also catch a glimpse of the extent of our sorrow, of lost friends and swallowed time, like being surprised by our own dark reflection in a plate glass window. Almost always we jump back, avert our eyes, knowing as we do the feeling we suppress: all the rivers in the world flooding our heart until it bursts, water welling from the corners of our eyes in a rain of tears. We stop, because we are merely human, and because otherwise we would weep forever.

From my birth I lived with chronic illness among my brothers. Now, as a gay man, I live with chronic illness once more — among my brothers. I share that illness. But what ails us is not just the virus that wends through our veins, insinuating itself in gland, node, lobe. What can kill us when AIDS infects us, what suffocates us when we deny the truth of AIDS around us, is what happens when we fail to embrace our lives in death and the death in life. That malady devastates us all. It is the enemy of love.

The Crisis of Desire

LOSS AND PROMISE

E VERY HUMAN INFECTED with HIV has a point of departure. I carry HIV because I am a gay man, and because in the early 1980s I lived in New York, Amsterdam, Berlin — all centers of the maelstrom. To journey back to those beginnings is to find the source of the crisis of desire that afflicts us now.

When I lived in Europe from 1980 to 1983, I filed stories on gay issues for North American magazines and eventually settled in West Berlin for six months. Living at the line where the two super-powers' spheres of influence abutted at a concrete barrier, I was fascinated by how the Berlin Wall divided lives, and especially how the river of male-male sexuality was diverted into such disparate streams. Here were two territories of exiles.

It was also while I was in West Berlin that I began to realize AIDS was going to be a far more serious problem than anyone had imagined. In May 1983 while I was visiting a local German friend, a gay traveler from New York City left his suitcase open on the living-room floor. On top of clothing was a pile of packaged condoms. I had thought of such devices as burdens that heterosexuals had to employ to avoid conception. I remember my shock, together with the sinking realization that apparently some people were really taking this "gay cancer" thing seriously.

At that same time I made contact with an emerging group of gay liberationists in communist East Berlin. In the Western sector with all its freedom, gay life seemed cynical, indifferent, and even bored with its own liberties; in the East, the people I met were vital, hospitable — and oppressed. While homosexuality was legal on both sides of the wall, in the East it was caught in a pre-Stonewall time warp. Men had sex with other men, but they were less likely to construct their identities around their desires. There was something out of time about sex east of the wall, something almost early adolescent, as if the men who cruised the streets for each other were too green to shape the words to describe what they knew they wanted. Sexual connection to them was risky, sexy, and precious. Yet Western concepts of sex were slowly seeping through. In 1983 the first rustlings of sexual-identity politics were being felt by East German gay men and lesbians, who nevertheless maintained an uneasy coexistence with the dominant sexual culture. An essay appeared in an "approved" — that is, ideologically correct — literary magazine that defended the right of homosexuals to live in a socialist system. This, I was told, could not have happened by accident. It was a sign, the first stirring of government sanction of gay people.

Organizing for gay rights was illegal in the German Democratic Republic, because any group that wasn't state sponsored was considered contrary to the interests of the proletariat. The only exceptions had been carved out within the body of the still-powerful Protestant Church. Certain dissident groups formed among the church membership as alternatives to state-sponsored or state-forbidden activities — a women's movement, an ecology movement, an antiwar movement. A gay liberation group had formed at the Protestant seminary in Leipzig in 1982 and had since spread to Berlin. On a sunny June day in 1983 in a church parish in Rummelsberg, a red brick suburb of East Berlin, at a "Peace Fair" sponsored by the Evangelische Kirche, I attended a public exhibition on homosexuality sponsored by East German gay and lesbian activists. It was the first public manifestation of gay liberation in the eastern sector of Berlin since Nazi troops burned the library of the League for Sexual Reform on a pyre in the Opern Platz in 1933.

There I met Bernd Schaubert, one of the most celebrated graphic designers in the GDR. Then in his mid-thirties, Bernd dressed like a punk rocker with a gay twist and was highly in demand as a creator of album covers and posters for East German rock bands. One of his "punk" album covers had been banned by the state. He had applied to emigrate to West Germany, an effort he said would take six years. He had been immediately dismissed from his union, which meant he could no longer work. "Firemen" — actually the secret police — paid midnight "inspections" to his little house on Muggelsee. He desperately wanted to get to the West. But as I had found to be true with many East Germans, in just a short conversation I saw that his vision of life in the West was highly idealized, one shaped by television and hopefulness, not experience.

As we took a train back downtown after the rally, a boy across the car carrying flowers began cruising Bernd, who looked back at him with furtive attentiveness. I watched the East German soldier who sat across from us, his girlfriend snuggled against his uniform. He in turn regarded Bernd and the boy with brutal suspicion. I felt he could rise to strike us or arrest us on a whim. And in that moment I felt a wave of disillusionment spill over me, mixed with terror, as if the soldier, or the smug and brutal force he represented, could suddenly rise up and smite us all. The precious, secret moment had turned pernicious.

East Berlin had a strange quality of impending disaster on those hot June nights. During my last visit there, I gazed out at the wing-spread imperial eagles along the Alte Museum, silhouetted by a blazing red sunset, and saw the hulking postures of vultures waiting for the corpse to cool. I wasn't sure what the corpse was, exactly —

East Germany? Or was it also the death of an innocence that comes from pre-identity, a colony that had somehow thrived unnoticed under the glare of the tyrant?

I met my last East German boy there. We walked arm in arm around Alexanderplatz to get drunk on *weisser* beer in the tavern in city hall. He grinned hungrily at me when he found out I was North American. We had sex up against the S-Bahn bridge at Marx-Engels-Platz, hidden by bushes. Just beyond us were the piping voices of boys fishing dirty fish in the Spree, and the lights on Museum Isle, transporting us to classical Greece. As I felt his body ravenous against mine, I realized I was not just a person to him, not even just a sex partner, but the physical incarnation of a world he dreamed of, a realm that shimmered and sparkled on the other side of a wall and a death zone, only a few blocks away. There are other forms of objectification than that which comes from admiring beauty. It didn't bother me to be objectified. If anything, to paraphrase Etty Hillesum as she spoke of her Dutch soldier-lovers in 1944, he was hungry; I fed him my body.

Although I'll never be completely certain, I think HIV passed to me that summer in West Berlin, from a man named Rollo, a skin-head punk rocker who sported a leather cord around his neck, owned a successful café, and lived in a squatter's house at the far end of Kreuzeberg, where his porcelain teacups sat amid a scaffolding of black steel stereo equipment. We met that June and became lovers. Rollo did not see any contradiction in being a well-to-do owner of a café who was also an antiestablishment punk, nor was he bothered that his squatter's quarters contained thousands of marks' worth of audio. Grand, devious, and a little silly, he bullied his contradictions into silence. He was also an ostentatiously sexual man, taking delight in danger. Once, when he had mounted me from behind and I was about to come, I abruptly felt his leather thong tighten around my neck. Rollo was cutting off my breath. Deprived of air, my nerves and muscles tensing and surrendering, I had an orgasm that was transcendent, a dance with darkness. By the time he let me breathe again, Rollo was laughing and holding me. I was limp with joy.

As much as I was fascinated with Rollo and his swagger, I had grown desperate to leave the hothouse that was Berlin. Its arid society unnerved me, left me aching to take a deep clean breath. I decided I would go to live in Paris for six months; someone had offered me an empty apartment I could use for the first five weeks. I had had to give up my room in Berlin starting September 1, but I couldn't travel to Paris for another seven days. An English friend, Martin, offered to let me stay in his apartment for the weekend. His roommate — the apartment's owner — was a man named Axel, an East German political prisoner who had spent five years in solitary confinement before being "bought" by the Bundesrepublik and brought to the West. Ransoming East Germans was a common practice for Bonn at that time. Axel walked with a permanent stoop. His leftism was far more radical than the institutional communism of the GDR. During my visit he would be going away for a left-wing "think tank" weekend at some seaside village. Martin stayed at his girlfriend's flat all the time. I went there on Friday to discover that the apartment had also been lent to a young Australian couple passing through Berlin on their way around the world. They took Martin's bedroom and I took the unused living room.

By Friday night I was feeling nauseated and had a growing fever. By Saturday morning it was definitely the flu, mysterious, severe, abrupt, out of season.

Also on Saturday morning the electricity went off. Axel, we found out, had forgotten to pay his bill and ignored the notices. The soonest it could be turned back on was Monday. No one had any money, but it was a major crisis for Martin and his girlfriend. As a result, they had to stop by constantly to make telephone calls. By Saturday afternoon I realized the ancient toilet, which I was using for both violent ends of my body, had rocked off its base, leaking vast quantities of filthy water every time it was flushed.

By the time Axel came home on Sunday evening, I was burning with fever and delirious at night. My body continued to reject everything I tried to put into it, even water. For the next two days I was only dimly aware of people entering the room, then leaving it. When I became conscious again, weak and still feverish, Axel was pacing the apartment, the fingers of one hand pursed at the bridge of his nose.

"Have I been bothering you?" I asked guiltily, aware of the degree to which I had overstayed his roommate's invitation.

Axel halted, as if suddenly distracted and forced to notice me. "Bother me?" he asked, surprised. "I'm thinking about Auschwitz, German history, the Berlin Wall — how can you possibly bother me!" He went on to explain that at the weekend retreat an unexpected issue had come up and taken over the agenda: Why was there no joy in left-wing politics anymore?

Axel went back to his thinking, furrowing his whiskery brow again and shaking his head stiffly as he muttered sternly, "There must be a way to have joy again . . ."

I was strong enough to walk to my friend Rick's apartment in a different neighborhood but nauseated again by the time I got there. Rick opened the door, sleepy-eyed and wearing pajama bottoms. "You look like hell," he said. "Baby, you're really sick, aren't you?" I nodded mutely. He reached for my arm and pulled me into the apartment. In one smooth motion he got dressed, put on his coat and hat, and led me by the hand to a doctor's office, where he easily persuaded the physician to use one of Rick's own health insurance certificates and examine me. The doctor prescribed a noxious brown liquid medicine that I took by the spoonful. Rick put me to bed. Overnight my fever broke in a sweat-filled dream, and the next morning I awakened better.

It wasn't until many years later that I recalled that September flu in Berlin, how inexplicable it was. By then I knew enough to know I was experiencing what gay men would now, as they grope the past to discover the moment when their lives turned on a pivot, call seroconversion illness. In about 70 percent of people, infection with HIV precipitates an often severe flulike sickness, which is the body's first furious attempt to master the virus as it assumes its place in the bloodstream, a visitor settling in to do its sinister work in silence, for a decade or so, until the body blossoms into visible disease.

Our crisis began with our disbelief, from the condoms in the suitcase to the first Kaposi's sarcoma lesion on the ankle. We were dumbfounded at a notion that even now seems incredible: that sex could cause cancer. As we realized the magnitude of the epidemic, we were horrified, angry, terrified, and pathologically depressed. Those states recur. Inured to the routine of this unending war, and with no real truce in sight, we can forget how much we've undergone and what the costs have been. In the nearly two decades we've lived with AIDS, our reaction to the epidemic has mutated as many times as the virus has. We've moved from denial and disbelief to fear, empowerment, action, sexualness, sexlessness, and fatigue.

From the start, AIDS laid siege to all the things that we homosexuals have created since Stonewall, from social and sexual freedom to the fragile edifice of a common history, to a degree of tolerance from the general population, and much of the expansive, balloon-frame gay community we had built up in a decade's time. The siege has been so relentless and subtle that we grew acclimated to death and deprivation behind the walls of the gay city. We have been persistent and gutsy in fabricating a shantytown of support services, activist efforts, and sex venues. Yet when it comes to comprehending what we have lost and the burdens we carry, we barely acknowledge our bruises, like a child who can imagine no other life than to be beaten by her father every evening.

By the time I returned to Canada in 1984 and saw my brother die, a former roommate was languishing in a hospital, supine and staring wordlessly at the ceiling. I insisted, wrongly, "He can't have AIDS, he's not emaciated or anything." On the phone for the first time in a long time with an ex-lover, the idle happy question "How ya' doin'?" was answered with a low, reluctant "Not so well, actually." A friend tells me that our friend has thrush in his throat. "Thrush? What's that?" Candidiasis. White patches in the mouth, a sign of a level of immune dysfunction that can swiftly descend into AIDS itself.

We had little medical reason to hope. In 1986 AZT was just making its tentative and overhyped entry onto the scene. Alternative therapies came and went every day — AL-721 spread on slices of bread, megadoses of vitamin C, macrobiotic diets, Saint Johnswort, piss. New opportunistic infections seem to arise weekly. The toll of deaths mounted exponentially, astonishingly. Money for research and treatment remained scarce; what funds existed were often ill allotted by a patronizing, socially tone-deaf medical establishment. With rising AIDS awareness came rising AIDS prejudice.

The virus itself would mutate, and the effect on the gay community would alter as well, with the discovery of HIV as the cause of AIDS, and the advent of HIV testing. Gone was the scary idea that AIDS could strike the "worried well," those gay men who thought they might be ambushed by the lightning of an opportunistic infection. By 1987 gay men could discover whether they were either HIV-positive or -negative; they knew their fates. It was as if two brothers were being sent to be reared in different homes, one in Beirut and one in Mayberry. The result was a swiftly erected wall between those who had to worry about survival and those who did not. Gone too was the distinction between people with AIDS and people who carried the virus or who had AIDS-related complex; now the story we were fed was that just about everybody who had been infected by the virus would get sick and die. It was no small wonder that gay men staggered through their lives drunk with sorrow. We have lived so long with AIDS that we can barely conceive of life without the confines of HIV, just as children coming of age in a city long under siege can imagine no diet except grass and clay.

If we are to figure out what we as gay men have become because of AIDS, we have to begin by acknowledging our loss. Some of the casualties are obvious — the lives of more than three hundred thousand gay men, much of an entire generation — but the devastation that AIDS has brought upon us is not measurable only through the bodies we have buried. Over time and through death after death, and even more recently in an era when hope exists that the worst of the loss is behind us, it is easy to avert our eyes from the enormous monotone of disaster. Only when we can step back just enough to survey the entire moonscape that is AIDS — from the first inexplicable deaths to the latest, inhibited hope, from the havoc in our bodies to the calamity it has caused to our culture, our sexuality, and our place in the world — can we know where we might still make a stand as creatures of human love and possibility.

What has AIDS done to us gay men?

Its virus has killed most of a generation of gay men: in America alone, nearly three hundred thousand of the four hundred thousand dead of AIDS are openly homosexual men.

It casts a shadow over another nine hundred thousand people, men and women and children, who are HIV-positive, in North America alone. And millions more in Africa, Asia, Europe, and South America.

It has made us mistrust our bodies, which can fail us before their time.

AIDS parted the HIV-positive from the HIV-negative; the infected from the infectable; those who are daily prompted by their mortality from those who can avert their eyes from that reminder; those who are more likely to die sooner from those who are likely to die later. It made us define ourselves through these differences.

It made us mistrust other men's bodies, which can betray us in spite of those men's best intentions.

For the most intimate and trusting of sexual touches, HIV has drawn between us a curtain of latex. It has denied us the conductive heat of another man's body. It has deadened sensation.

For the most intimate and trusting of emotional touches, it has dropped a drape between us that is thicker than latex: gay men who never felt legitimate in their own bodies now had reason not to trust other men or other men's bodies.

It took from us men who were skilled at loving.

It absconded with the men who had first embodied our sexuality — those Stonewall veterans, those seventies queens and Radical Faeries and manic activists — who knew where we had been and could have charted where we could go. Vito Russo, Robert Chesley, Bill Kraus, Marty Robinson, Michael Lynch, Paul Monette, Dorian Corey, George Stambolian, Robert Ferro, Michael Grumley, Michael Callen, Robert Massa, Tom Stoddard — all are lost to us.

AIDS denied younger men the wisdom, sexual and generational, of older men. Those men who died of AIDS at age forty in 1982 — what would they have learned that would have told the rest of us how to grow old, to be adult, to wear our well-worn bodies like a badge? And the lovers and friends who survive those men: their veteran grief teaches us much, but if they had not been so preoccupied with loss, where else could they have led us? What paths, once blazed for us, have grown over with grief?

AIDS has devastated gay men of color whose parallel lives, diverse identities, and fierce, enlarged numbers would have created an even more distinct and vital community intertwining race and sexuality, and whose numbers would have given greater complexity to the frozen vanilla yogurt of contemporary urban gay sexuality. AIDS silenced Asotto Saint, David Frechette, Melvin Dixon, Essex Hemphill, Steven Corbin, Marlon Riggs.

AIDS stirred resentment among lesbians and straight women who chose to care for men with AIDS and their causes — often to the detriment of their own, and often without proper gratitude or reciprocal support from gay men and heterosexuals. In the quest for scarce medical resources and limited human sympathy, AIDS forced white gay men to compete with HIV-affected people of other races, classes, sexes, and sexualities. At a time when the world of power ignored us, we were set against each other even as we tried, in our wary and angry ways, to come together.

AIDS has denied many gay men the chance even to consider the option of begetting children.

AIDS has made gay men so afraid of our bodies — those frail and temporal constructions — that many of us have girded ourselves in the armor of muscle. It is no coincidence that the explosion of the urban physique culture in the early 1980s occurred as the virus burst into visibility on our skins. Before 1980, gay men could thrive in the gay public square and be happily slender, more sylph than sculpture. Now, more than we acknowledge, if a thin man is over twenty-five and his cheekbones are sharp, we believe that his body could harbor virus.

AIDS spawned other systems of guilt and denial, from the happy blame systems of New Age guru Louise Hay to recreational party drugs that help us ignore our losses. Illegal drugs are the guerrilla comrade of HIV; the virus often infiltrates the body when men, drugged, slipping into carelessness, let their guards slip. Though such party favors have been with us since the 1960s, today they serve the purpose of reiterating the physical, grounding us in happy body sensations when we might spin off into anxiety. Overheard at a white party at the Saint in New York, Sunday around noon, one shirtless partier speaking to another, who is weeping: "Come on, honey. The memorial service isn't until four o'clock. You've got time for another hit. You'll feel better. Really."

AIDS reminded us we were sexual outlaws in America. Having created enclaves of independence — the disdainful call them ghettos — where for the first time in human history we could choose to live lives in the open, we now had to crawl to hospitals, the FDA, the news media, the research lab, and the parents we left behind. Some of those parents took us in and loved us; some people in the media and the medical establishment cared or learned to care. AIDS made us supplicants.

AIDS has told the heterosexual world that we are predatory, sexually poisonous.

AIDS has also told gay men we are predatory, sexually poisonous. Like hard-drinking street fighters who convert vehemently to born-again Christianity, many gay men have believed what AIDS has told them about their bodies.

AIDS did not even stay news. The astounding fact of half a million dead people, as many as 37,500 still dying every year, became as newsworthy as male pattern baldness.

AIDS would deny us the adventure of gay male multipartner sexuality, however safe and self-aware, and penalize those who would try, through their thoughts or their sexual journeying, to build a new network of roads for intimate human connections.

AIDS is not entirely a total rout, of course. Gay men have come together in brotherhood; people have cared for each other heroically and lived with valor under a siege so insidious it masquerades as daily life. In spite of AIDS and because of it, the rights of gay men and lesbians have advanced, even as the Catholic Church and the religious-right establishment beat them back with their Neolithic arguments. More and more gay men are coming out of the closet, negotiating the straits of contemporary gay male sexuality even as some risk shipwreck, confronting addictions, absence of intimacy with boyfriends and sex partners, seroconversion, and persistent, queasy fear. The cloud that is AIDS has its tin lining.

AIDS would wither the promise of our bodies.

Perhaps most profound of all for both the worried well and the soon to die, AIDS threatened the very thing that defined gay men: gay desire. In bedrooms and back rooms alike, with a crafty virus afoot, we no longer knew how to have sex with each other, or what sex meant to us. Should a man just find a lover and hunker down, content or desperate, until the storm blew past? Would a positive man have sex with a negative one? If so, what were the responsibilities of each partner? The questions were at once practical and existential. What did safer sex mean, both in terms of the exchange of bodily fluids and in terms of emotional risk? In what way could it once again be a radical and life-engendering act to connect sexually with another man?

Desire became infused with fear. In the mid-1980s and beyond, we did not know how to have sex with each other. "I remember coming to New York in 1982 and being terrified," says Calvin, a friend of mine. "First it was herpes, which everyone said was the worst thing that could ever happen to you. Then it was AIDS, and nobody knew how you got it or how you stayed safe from it. The health people were telling us to shower with your partners to see if they had any bruises — Kaposi's sarcoma — but before long we learned that advice was pretty silly. I remember one New Year's Eve meeting a guy in some basement peepshow on Christopher Street and letting him suck my dick for ten seconds before I went limp. I went home and was convinced I'd killed myself. Ten seconds!"

HIV warps how we enter into relationships with each other. I know many men who have tethered themselves into couples and tried to withdraw from the possibility of infection. Some of those couples survive. Others ultimately dissolve, because an awareness of an inappropriate choice overcomes their fear of the outside world. Certain sets of lovers withdrew into what they thought was safety and had to face HIV anyway, when one or both of them discovered his preexisting HIV-positive status or else seroconverted. Increasingly, some young men have come to fear the plague less in practice than in the abstract: it is something that has killed their big brothers, not them. That attitude means, in practice, that many of those men are getting infected in their twenties and early thirties — just like their big brothers.

In 1983, I believed I had nothing to fear from Rollo. Since then, one slip, one mistake in judgment, one too many bumps of crystal meth, one penis thrashing in the wrong place, once, and our fates change. It's hard to risk intimacy when you already feel like you're risking your life.

For one breath in human history, desire was not wrapped up in death. For perhaps two generations, from the end of the Second World War until 1982, the collision of bodies was a means and metaphor of human freedom, not risk.

My parents came of age before that era, and they paid a price. During the war, my mother was in training as a nurse at a Catholic hospital. Trainees were forbidden to marry, but she was engaged to a man who had emigrated from Germany in the early 1930s and at the outbreak of war joined the Canadian navy. In the fall of 1943, he came home on embarkation leave. His ship was sailing from Halifax in two weeks. They eloped. A few months later he died in a sea battle, barely weeks before my mother was to graduate. The nuns who ran the hospital were about to expel her but relented; for punishment, despite the exigency of war, she was not allowed to receive her diploma in the ceremony with her classmates, and she was not listed as a graduate. A year later, the war was over, and all the young men returned. As a widow, my mother found herself ostracized.

It is another pernicious myth of the patriarchal system: because a widow was no longer a virgin, she was seen by men as a ready sexual possibility, and by other women as too much competition.

In the fall of 1939, at the age of seventeen, my father lied about his age and joined the Canadian army. He spent six years in England and Europe, returning home when he was twenty-three to marry his former high school sweetheart. Needless to say, it was a disaster. At that time the only ground for divorce was adultery. He paid a detective to take photographs of him in a hotel room with another woman, and gave the photographs to his wife so she could go to court. In the meantime, he met my mother and they dated. She became pregnant. Abortion was forbidden. My father's divorce wasn't final. They did what any other self-respecting couple with an out-of-wedlock pregnancy did in those days: they went away, thousands of miles from everyone they knew, to have the baby. All they had in common was a single recessive gene for cystic fibrosis.

After a brief pretend honeymoon in Chicago, they ended up in Nova Scotia, where my brother Christopher was born. Six months later, they finally married. It was a secret they kept successfully from their children for more than thirty years, until the last week of my brother's life, when it finally came out during the trauma of Chris's dying.

The disquieting story of the origins of their marriage is not that unusual for their generation; it illustrates how the young men and women then were trapped, not only by the Great Depression, and the Second World War, but by all the legislative and institutional rules, not to mention social mores, that controlled their lives. They were denied life choices because of the tyranny of an archaic moral system. Having undergone the trials of war and endured social oppression, the parents of the baby-boom generation demanded control from church and state over their reproductive decision-making.

My parents and their children encouraged and witnessed medical, technological, social, and legal advances that allowed women and men greater autonomy over their bodies. Contraception became commonplace and abortion became legal. Antibiotics and vaccines rendered most sexually transmitted diseases treatable. For the first time ever, men and women were relieved of the burden of health risks in their sexual decision-making. Anticensorship decisions opened up the agora of ideas. Sex education grew more prevalent. In political rhetoric the new autonomy was expressed in many ways, from the "Black is beautiful" chants of black liberation, to the "Hell no, we won't go!" of the anti–Vietnam War movement, to the feminist creed, "Our bodies, ourselves," to gay liberation's analysis of self-oppression: "The liberation of the homosexual can only be the work of homosexuals themselves," as the early sex radicals told us.

By 1970, the feminist, gay liberation, and the earlier civil rights movements were a troika. They created a politics of the body by challenging political structures and moral strictures of race, gender, and desire that had controlled human beings for millennia. It was the culmination of a centuries-long trend from a morality based on procreation to one that permitted sex for recreation and embraced sex itself as generative. The right to determine sexual values was taken back from historical institutions and given to the individual.

Lesbians and gay men were on the vanguard of that battle: to reconstruct desire based not on the code society dictated but on the authenticity of the desires of a single human being. Pioneering a culture based on the veracities of desire was daunting work. How did we know how a woman would relate to other women without the constraints of preconceived sexual power, or how a man might honestly and equitably connect with other men? We had no idea then; we still have little. The liberation of the body remains a task to be accomplished by heroes. It is exploration begun at dawn, when the shape of the frontier remains unclear.

The work of these liberationists has been twofold: to reconnect the individual with the authenticity of his own character, and to bring that individual into the genuine embrace of others.

The inexplicably personal experience of homosexual liberation, of "coming out," crossing the shame-enforced line of taboo to self-realization, was repeated countless times throughout the Western world. Taking what they could from the general women's movement, lesbians discovered in their own way what gay men were finding on male-male terrain: that every time a homosexual man stepped across the line out of shame, he became aware not only that he had been forced to repress his sexual expression, but that the act of repression had stunted every aspect of his being — his emotions, creativity, spirituality. So, like energy released from nuclear fusion, the collective experience of "coming out" could be an implosion of extraordinary primal energy, one that a generation of gay men and lesbians used to build a political movement and international community in less than a decade.

Their idealism held that sexual relations were central to the task of changing and improving all human relations: the vision of a Marcusian utopia where Freud embraced Marx. Freed from repression, the libido embraced anarchy instead of aggression. What better way to end all war than for battling armies of men to lie down with each other in coitus! For gay men, their new lives beckoned with the same mystery and excitement as the challenge of space, the secrets of the atom, or the philosophical implications of relativity.

Prizing the act of sex from myths of romance and nuclear families, we began to develop new models for our relationships. There was certainly idealism, but it was not just theoretical; we were changing our lives, rewriting the script that history and culture had handed us.

In a small town in Manitoba at the age of twelve, I stood in front of a bedroom mirror, examining my changing body. I was finally connecting the whispered warnings or sharp derision of homosexuality to the desires that had suffused me since the age of four or five. The first stirrings of my sexuality at the very beginning of my adult life left me a permanent pariah. They condemned my life to hell. I was sixteen when Canada's laws against homosexuality were repealed — when an erstwhile bachelor Minister of Justice named Pierre Trudeau removed them from the criminal code. I was lucky; I came of age at a time when I could find air to breathe. In my early twenties, when the light of liberation flooded into my own life and I recharacterized myself as gay, I stepped from the self-exile of the closet, a life of inner duplicity, to claim my body's own primacy. By embracing my real nature, I had a sense I could join the world on my own terms, after having long lived at its periphery.

But coming to terms with having AIDS — coming out with AIDS — is like stepping back to the periphery. This time, the exile is not from the self, but from everyone whose blood is not yet poison, from that group of human beings — in fact, the vast majority of humanity — who have not murdered, or been murdered by, their lovers.

Rollo and I corresponded a little for a few years, lost touch. Then in 1987 I received a post card demanding, "Are you still alife?" There was another exchange, then silence.

I have never been back to Berlin, and for many years I did not return to Europe at all. In early 1989 and 1990 I visited Amsterdam and Paris. In Amsterdam I discovered that another former lover, Hans, had been sick for several months. In Paris, I knew that some friends were already dead: Vladimir, a poet; Guy Hocquenghem, the gay theorist; Copi, the cartoonist and playwright. I wrote ahead to others — Alain, Bernard, Thierry, Peter — to tell them I was coming, and on arrival went in search of them. From my hotel room I telephoned. No one answered endless rings, or lines were no longer in service.

At Le Louvre des Antiquaires I stepped into Alain's shop and saw that all the items on sale were from the wrong century. An earnest woman, the new owner, told me he was *"décédé"* — for a year now. Yes, of course it was AIDS. All of Alain's friends were dead too. "New York *a flambé tout*," she concluded brightly. New York really fucked everything up.

Bernard had lived in an apartment on the Rue de Rivoli. There a wizened concierge pursed her lips and said, *"Il est décédé."* She shrugged off further questions with a typical Parisian brusqueness. An elegantly dressed older woman stepped into the courtyard from the interior of the building, her eyes glancing quickly at me, indicating she had overheard. I turned to her and asked the same questions: Was it AIDS? Of course. When? What happened to Peter, Bernard's lover? She didn't know.

I told her of my day in Paris. She looked at me sadly, but with something more — concern and even recognition. *"C'est comme la guerre,"* she said grimly. It's like war. And I knew exactly what she meant: I was like a soldier or prison camp survivor returning to my ruined neighborhood, not knowing who survived and who did not, where to find someone, or even where to find out where he might have gone.

I left Paris to visit Gilles, another friend, in the south of France. When I greeted him in Perpignan, he told me that a month earlier his tongue had turned white with thrush — the first sign of impending disease. A week later, when I returned in New York, I found that the letter I sent to Thierry in Paris before leaving had been returned by the French post office, stamped *"Décédé."*

By 1991 Hans was dead. In 1992, a simple note in the mail informed me that Gilles was gone. My life in Europe, the friends and faces who peopled my days there, had burned out; my memories, like great networks of power lines, were cast into darkness.

In Berlin, the wall had come down, and in 1990 an East Berlin friend named Bruno visited me in New York City. Only seven years earlier, at a birthday party at his apartment on Schonhauser Allee, we'd agreed that the wall would likely exist for our entire lives. The night it was opened, Bruno told me, he had attended the premiere of the first explicitly gay feature film made in East Germany. The essay in the approved literary journal in 1983 had been the opening of a steady acceptance of gay people by the socialist government. Now the socialist state had ceased to exist, and the strange, time-warped gay community of East Berlin was being swallowed by the West — and apparently by AIDS.

Bruno brought news of Bernd Schaubert, the graphic designer. The GDR authorities had deported him to West Germany in 1985. But someone like him, a prominent professional in the East, went to the bottom of the career ladder in West Berlin. Bernd found life there disillusioning and finally wrote to the GDR government requesting permission to return. The government passed the letter along to the communist daily newspaper, which printed it in full; it was perfect propaganda for a state that had turned the entire country into a walled prison. Permission was denied. Bernd's exodus to the West ended in ignominy. A year or so later, he died from AIDS in a West Berlin hospital.

Many years ago I read of the life of Klaus Mann, Thomas Mann's son who wrote the novel *Mephisto*, the film version of which won an Oscar in 1982. Klaus Mann fled the Nazis to America, survived the Second World War working as a translator for the American army, and was one of the first liberators to enter Berlin. In 1946, he walked into an Austrian cemetery, put a gun into his mouth, and blew his head off. Before AIDS and even in the epidemic's early years that I wanted so much to survive, I was baffled by his final act: Why would someone who had survived when so many others had not choose to end it all so abruptly? Similarly, I had been puzzled by the high suicide rate among Jewish Holocaust survivors. By the late 1980s, with a dozen friends dead, I understood: the world Klaus Mann had known had been destroyed, gone forever. He had no desire to live in the new one rising from the ashes. He knew he could never belong to it, and made a choice to leave it. That is one choice we have — not to rebuild the charred city but to exile ourselves from its ruins.

Whenever I tell straight men or women that I am infected with HIV, they show concern about my health and then almost always surmount their embarrassment to ask me how I got it. This question preoccupies heterosexuals far more than gay men, since straight people are even more prone to swallow the social and medical myths of blame and recrimination around HIV infection, and see HIV not as something you live with but just die from. For all the shame many of us wear like a lead apron, gay men are far less interested in figuring out how we were infected. Certainly, given the amount of sex we have had, we often don't know who could have passed on the virus to us; it could have happened a hundred different times, and for some it did. Some of us knew exactly even in the beginning, as the late writer David Feinberg declared in his last book, *Queer and Loathing:* "I can pinpoint the precise moment when I was infected with HIV (August 12, 1982, at approximately 1:47 in the morning in some seedy establishment best left to the imagination)." Also, many of us know with some certainty that we have been infected by a lover — or have infected him, tossing the virus back and forth like a hand grenade.

Even in the age of safer-sex guidelines, when men often can determine what "slip" happened to them when they were drunk or in bed with a lover and just went too far, we seldom blame the other man. Often, even when we have slipped up sexually, we do not blame ourselves. There has been no gay Kimberly Bergalis, the young Florida woman who claimed to have been infected by her dentist and who became a cause célèbre in the late 1980s, the "innocent victim" brought up to Washington, D.C., on her deathbed to testify before Senator Jesse Helms and seek sanctions for HIV-positive health workers. Gay men do not necessarily feel guilty for having the virus, but they do not feel innocent, either. Gay men in the eighties, and even gay men now, have generally felt implicated in HIV transmission, as if getting the virus were an inevitability, a risk of being sexual. This attitude can be dangerously fatalistic, as psychologist Walt Odets has discussed in his book *In the Shadow of the Epidemic*: "Many men with consistent negative test histories and safer sex behavior to match do not believe they will survive. Patients often say they *know* they are uninfected but *feel like* or *believe* they are positive — or will, somehow, inevitably become so."

But our integration of the fact of HIV infection in our lives can suggest the bond among us, the shared recognition that none of us is immune. Some of those gay men who emerged uninfected from the early years of the epidemic may possess a genetic twist that kept them resistant to the virus; most other uninfected men, however conservative their sexual practices, were just lucky. Infected or not, gay men tend to recognize they are still part of the HIV brotherhood. If some in the tribe have the disease, then all of us do — or so we think, at our best. We are connected in a web of illness, love, and fear. Thus love and death spin their waltz.

I have chosen to think that Rollo is my murderer, but I attach no blame to him. I only love his memory more. Everyone was ignorant then. It was no fault of his. It could have just as easily been me, because I'm certain that in those years of ignorance, through no intention of my own, I was a bringer of disease to other men.

Hearing the story of Rollo wrapping his leather thong around my neck, some people will take it as a fearsome and tragic metaphor, the outward and visible sign not just of a fate unwittingly delivered but of a life already half in love with easeful death. The HIV transmission that occurred that day was tragic, or, like the transmission of cystic fibrosis or a cancer diagnosis, at least unfortunate; no one should have to die young. Those people are right that my dance with Rollo is a metaphor. I ask, however, that they consider that moment with something approaching awe. I very much regret that I have HIV. I do not regret for an instant the intense, connective, vivid, enlivening sex I had with Rollo.

That gay men cannot separate Rollo from his virus has caused us untold trouble. AIDS has made us afraid of both sex and death. HIV has entwined death and desire. Because we have not yet learned to wriggle in between them, like a child crawling between his parents in the marital bed, we suffer from a crisis of the sexual heart.

Most of us, even those of us who die of AIDS, are ultimately survivors. In the long cold war that is AIDS, it is possible that we can rise to the crisis, seeking to advance the potential of the gay body in inventive, generative ways. Even as I lament our losses and probe our injuries, I aim to see what we might yet build, based upon the command we retain of our bodies' livelihoods. We have demanded authority over the medical treatments that go into our bodies, thanks to ACT UP and its offspring in the late 1980s and 1990s. We have assumed control over the means of the body's dying, as my friend Hans did in Amsterdam, in my presence. We still have sex, lots of us, even if some of it is threesomes with Mr. Bones.

Our gay vocation is not yet fulfilled. We can still take to heart those ideals that emancipated so many people a generation ago and reshape them for a new and virulent era, opening ourselves up once more to the promise of new forms of human authenticity. Our sexuality still gasps for air. We are like those hungry men to whom I gave myself in East Berlin, feverish and urgent and sexual as they strove to orgasm beneath the thick hand of the state. Under the oppression of HIV, we still can thrive, making ourselves rich with desire. Today the wall divides us not from material prosperity or even health but from our truest and most generous desires. It will not soon fall. How might we scale it, so as once again to touch desire eye to eye? How might we embrace Rollo?

Hope Inhibited

MEDICINE, POWER, AND THE RECLAIMED BODY

CLIFF DRANK HIS OWN urine every day for months. He began by mixing it with orange juice at breakfast, but eventually he drank it straight from the glass. Urine is full of antibodies, your own, excreted daily in the sterile medium of pee. Drinking it, the theory goes, infuses them back into your immune system. Cliff assured me that his KS lesions, tiny purple paisleys on his arms and neck, had shrunk a little. Cliff is dead.

Vito Russo's last lover, a handsome young guy named Jeffrey, returned to New York from a weekend New Age healing retreat in the Catskills. "I'm cured!" he announced, bursting in the door of Vito's apartment. He headed straight for kitchen, and a moment later we heard the sound of medication bottles tossed into the garbage. Vito rolled his eyes. Jeffrey appeared in the kitchen door, holding out a green trash bag filled with all his medications. "I don't need any of this anymore. I'm cured." He's dead too, and Vito outlived him by many years.

As AIDS defoliated the landscape of the 1980s, New Age blandishments promised healing through the resolution of life dilemmas, and succeeded mainly in making people feel like spiritual failures when their disease continued to progress. "Germ theory also works," as filmmaker Arthur Bressan, Jr., pointed out to me, more aware of the ironies than Jeffrey was, but just as full of hope. Artie's cramped apartment on West 15th Street in New York came to look like the lair of a mad scientist. The refrigerator held little round petri dishes containing custardlike AL-721, an egg lipid protein from Israel that was said to make HIV slip and slide off the surface of a T cell instead of attaching itself. Just like the first wave of men on the FDA-approved antiviral AZT, he awakened at 4 A.M. in order to take his lipid doses exactly six hours apart; he claimed the stuff was palatable if you ate it with strawberries. A friend of his brought over a Reichian orgone box and left it in his tiny kitchen. The box was the size and shape of a telephone booth, lined with burnished sheets of perforated copper. Wilhelm Reich, an iconoclast and exile from the field of psychoanalysis, claimed it cured cancer by concentrating certain cosmic rays; he died in jail, imprisoned by the Food and Drug Administration. But by May 1987, AL-721 wasn't doing whatever it was supposed to do for Artie, and the orgone box sat dusty in the corner of his kitchen. Every time Artie Bressan swallowed he felt excruciating pain in his esophagus. He made his final arrangements, sent away his friends, and quietly took pills, alone, at home.

No one I'm aware of improved from injections of puréed fetal calf at a chic Swiss clinic for five thousand dollars a crack; nor did anyone thrive on ozone therapy, said gas bubbling through the blood supposedly to sweep up disease-progressing free radicals. I knew a couple of men who went directly downhill after that. Rock Hudson flew to Paris for HP23, the wonder drug of 1985, and died three months later. Perry Ellis, rumor has it, injected himself with household bleach, since it was known to kill HIV, as does gasoline.

Even when AZT became available, Cliff and my friend Timo

and others rejected it, not only out of concern for its efficacy but because it came from the same hand that was killing them. No one in the 1980s trusted the government or pharmaceuticals, and no one should have; no one should today, either. My friend Jay and Hans did take AZT, to no effect — on the virus, anyway. But their bodies grew thin, their muscle deteriorated, their hands and feet in perpetual pain from peripheral neuropathy. After three years on AZT (AZT taken by itself is almost useless, we now know, because after eighteen months HIV mutates to inure itself against it), Ron tried experimental DDI. It came in a powdered form, in a buffer that aggravated the diarrhea many AIDS patients already endured. The dose was twice as high as currently recommended. Ron was one of eight Americans who developed pancreatitis from DDI. He went into a coma and died in hospital within five days — before his doctor even got around to seeing him there.

The 1980s were the darkest, scariest years of the epidemic, when everything we tried we tried in the dark, and no matter what we did to master our bodies they slipped inexorably away from us. Although the Concord Study, showing that people on AZT lived no longer than those who did nothing, was not released until the summer of 1993, it was evident to the naked eye that friends on AZT soon withered away as quickly as friends who withered away holistically. Slowly, however, a kind of organized and aggressive hope began to reemerge as people did in fact start to live longer. They were surviving not because gay men started loving themselves the way Louise Hay and other gurus told them to; nor did they benefit from some grand theory of antiviral therapy descended to heal the masses. They were lasting longer not because of new developments in medicine but because alternative, cast-off, and off-label therapies became standardized as word spread among people living with AIDS and their organizations.

People stopped dying of pneumocystis pneumonia because they prophylaxed with Bactrim, dapsone, or pentamidine, existing drugs long ignored by the medical establishment. The idea of immuno-modulators, agents that could strengthen the immune system, had been ignored by American research, which was focused on a "kill the virus" strategy. New alternative therapies began to appear so quickly that they were referred to derisively as "drug of the month." Most disappeared after an initial flurry of excitement; a few, how-ever, stayed around because they seemed to work for some people. The evidence was purely empirical and anecdotal: who among your friends was dying, and who was not. Chinese traditional medi-cine became consistently popular because it actually seemed to work. Theorizing that AIDS wasting was nothing more than mal-nutrition from the body's inability to absorb nutrients, treatment activists began to research nutrition. They discovered that science knows much more about animal nutrition than human nutrition: domestic animals are profitable only when they're healthy, while humans are profitable when they're sick.

An entire movement of gray market buyers' clubs was estab-lished to import unlicensed drugs from other countries. Many of those drugs were shown to have significant benefits, though they were not at the time even examined by researchers, much less authorized by the FDA. Men like Martin Delaney, who founded Project Inform, began by passing suitcases of drugs at secret meet-ings in parking lots near the Mexican border. Getting drugs into the bodies of gay men with AIDS meant borrowing subterfuges from the Cold War spy movies of our collective youth.

Slowly, by the early 1990s, our expectations for life after an AIDS diagnosis began to broaden, but few of the agents responsible came from the grand research labs that received hundreds of millions of dollars from the gay community and the government to fight AIDS. These remedies filtered out of the offices of a few deter-mined doctors who found new ways to use old drugs. They came from AIDS treatment activists who read until they knew as much as the scientists. And they arrived in America from the illegal and defiant buyers' clubs that smuggled drugs like Compound Q and ribavirin into the country.

Public credit for the extension of life expectancy conveniently goes to science, when the real heroes are the AIDS treatment activists and doctors in private practice whose treatment decisions were far ahead of the data produced by official trials. Anyone who takes a careful look at what healthy people with HIV have been using to stay well in recent years will find that the list ranges from Bactrim to Chinese herbs, and that almost everything has been in use for fifty to five thousand years. AZT, whose value is dubious at best, was synthesized in 1961; the antiviral acyclovir and the toxic antiblindness drug DHPG were developed in the 1970s.

If you discount all the nucleoside analogue knockoffs — the alphabet soup of DDI, DDC, D4T, 3TC inspired by AZT — then arguably as late as fifteen years into the epidemic the entire armamentarium was based on forty-year-old technologies. It was not until 1995 that the first batch of truly "new" antivirals appeared from the pharmaceutical industry: protease inhibitors. Treatment activists and scientists have identified eleven weak spots on the virus that might be foci for attack by designer drugs. At the attack rate of one a decade — reverse transcriptase inhibitors in the eighties, protease inhibitors in the nineties — scientists appear to have a backlog that will provide funding for their labs for seven or eight decades.

Meanwhile, people with AIDS and HIV continue to go about their business of reinventing medicine and forging an entire new way to approach illness. At great cost, alone, and with many false turns and many, many deaths, the diseased pariahs of American society — gay men with HIV, hemophiliacs, injection drug users, women, and especially women and men of color — have shown the world how to take charge of the human *corpus*. In the face of an implacable virus and an impassive nation, a new fraternity of gay men arose, united not just by sexuality but by an elemental desire to save their own lives and help others — gay and straight — do the same. We've gone deeper into our bodies than we ever have before.

The poet James Merrill wrote, "All day from high within the skull — / Dome of a Pantheon, trepanned — light shines / into the body." Perhaps that light takes on a soft, red glow from molecules of iron, binding oxygen into the blood in hemoglobin. If we could fit into the space between the body's molecules — and bodies are mostly space, more water than solid matter — and manifest ourselves somehow at the intracellular level, we would float in a warm, pulsating, rose-colored, liquid world, the heartbeat like a kettledrum, torrents of blood susurrating through kid-glove vessels.

The plasma is aswirl with traffic: capsules and bullet-shaped objects, long zigzagging chains, pellets, and what appear to be Easter eggs. These are bacteria. Some are harmless, others not. Even smaller than bacteria are stranger objects. Some look like bent sticks; others are a small army of spheres, marching tightly in perfect rows like Nazi soldiers; still more are starbursts bristling with molecular arms; others are fish-shaped, bubble-shaped, balls clumped together and covered with fur. These are viruses, stray bits of genetic material, debris left over from the work of making nature. They are the link between being and inanimate matter, sometimes invidiously hostile to life.

Sudden and abrupt violence enters this dreamlike world, even as we float like a mote of dust in a warm beam of reddish light. A macrophage rears up, looking much like a sandworm from *Dune*. It shifts the bulges of its nondescript form into a yawning mouth, encircling as it does a bullet-shaped bacterium, drawing it into its giant maw, digesting it.

A T-4 cell glides past, a gelatinous ball. Deep inside it, like a brain floating in oil, sits its dark nucleus. But all is not well there: the cell is full of nutrient deficiencies, with low levels of zinc and selenium, B-12, and other important vitamins. Free radicals —

atoms of oxygen, each stripped of an electron, toxic slag from the body's cell factory — are ripping at the cell walls, damaging the long, intricate molecular necklaces of floating amino acids. Many of the T-4 cells are limp, their membranes thin from a lack of cholesterol, drooping from low levels of glutathione and L-carnitine and a dozen other chemicals whose biochemical dance fuels our daily life. Like a sour smell, molecules of tumor necrosis factor float past in herds with alarming frequency.

A little farther away floats an entire clump of T cells, stuck together like a cluster of grapes, wrinkled and withered. Inside their murky membranes are distorted nuclei, surrounded by rapidly replicating DNA. This clump of dying T cells is called syncitia. It is an indication of HIV infection.

The human immunodeficiency virus is easy to identify when it finally comes barreling along: it is a spheroid bristling with projections, like a Second World War sea mine, or a sputnik with lopped-off arms. As a result of the work of evolution, the little keys that stud the virus precisely fit certain molecules on the outer walls of human T cells. Several virions move along the edge of the cell, which floats serenely in the body's glow. The virions are tiny, like little ships docking along the coast of a great continent. The keys lock onto a protein arm extending from the cell.

Once attached, they're like a row of peas, polite in a pod. Twisted coils of ribonucleic acid explode from each HIV virion into the T cell's plasma, the clusters writhing like worms escaping a tin can. When the RNA wriggles inside, it relies on the protein enzyme reverse transcriptase (the target of AZT and its relatives) to produce viral DNA. The viral DNA is then integrated into the cell's nuclear DNA. That renders the cell an HIV factory. The cell now produces new RNA, which is used to make all of the components of a new human immunodeficiency virus. Tiny globes, each containing a virion, form along the inside of the cell wall. When they penetrate the membrane, they float away like bubbles into the dense traffic of the blood to the next collision with a T cell. Immediately the chemical transformation begins anew. Eaten up from the inside out, T cells fall together in syncitiac clumps, all of them manufacturing HIV. They are useless blobs choking up the constant transformations of chemicals that give us life.

If this body is that of a person aware of his seropositive status, we might glimpse AZT or another nucleoside analogue drug swaggering through the blood too, crystalline, like a Cardassian space ship, all points and glinting, jagged edges. When it comes across a chain of reverse transcriptase molecules, it attacks, locking on the chain and shutting its molecules down. But never all of them. Virions will continue to reproduce and eventually spawn mutations. HIV will do well in this AZT-riddled blood: its reverse transcriptase is quite probably no longer susceptible to AZT or some of its cousins.

However, there may exist in the bloodstream other chemical foes that HIV must face, ones that are more potent than AZT because they are specifically suited to the task of shutting down the virus. These are the protease inhibitors. HIV protease is an enzyme that serves as the "scissors" that clip HIV into its respective pieces after one of the body's cells has produced a new copy of the virus. The pieces are then assembled to form a fully functioning virus. Because of its key role in HIV replication, drug developers targeted this enzyme, and new drugs have been custom-designed to try to stop its work. These drugs lock down the enzyme, in an action similar to jamming a stone between the scissors blades. In the cells in which protease is active, long pieces of protein float like debris, waiting to be cut in precise ways so that a new virus can be assembled. But the protease inhibitor prevents this process and the viral protein is eventually degraded, its constituent pieces reused for the body's more healthy, normal metabolic purposes.

Yet the specter of mutation is also a problem with protease inhibitors, so the current conventional wisdom is to hit the virus with potent "cocktails" of three or more drugs. The battle is being waged on multiple fronts, with the nucleoside analogues (such as AZT) blocking the enzyme reverse transcriptase, while the protease inhibitors thwart protease. Thus two blockades occur. They operate on different sides of the infectious process. Nucleoside analogues seek to stop a virus from producing material that can be integrated into the cell's nucleus, which would lead the cell to become an HIV factory. Protease inhibitors try to sabotage the final assembly that occurs once such a factory exists.

It is a battle of Herculean effort, in which billions of T cells and billions of viruses confront one another every day. The chemical meddling of modern medicine is primitive compared to the body's own magnificent mechanisms, but perhaps such drugs will prove enough to tilt the field in the body's favor.

Over time, the body's immune response will actually assist HIV in replicating. Tumor necrosis factor, its production a naturally occurring phenomenon in an immune response to viruses, serves to enhance HIV in its infectious cycle. The virus can thrive and hide in certain parts of the body. The gut is a favored place for HIV to live, and the brain too; the virus sequesters itself in lymph nodes, in the thymus and adrenal glands — seemingly impervious even to protease inhibitors — and it begins to alter their architecture, to burn them out. For years this is hardly noticeable. Humans come with billions of spare parts.

When those spare parts run out, the body begins to die in various ways. HIV, a parasite, has been unsuccessful in developing a symbiotic relationship with human beings. When the host dies, the virus goes with it. Perhaps that is why the folk myth of "ripeness" has arisen. This romanticizing notion holds that as a gay man gets closer to the point where his body begins to crash, he becomes more and more handsome, his sexual draw greater as the virus seeks to send its progeny on through semen to another private galaxy of flesh and blood.

These virions are emperors, each and every one. They command vast legions of scientists. They swallow sorrow like water.

I want to tell a story of a hole in atmospheric ozone, because the idea of ozone disappearing into a hole comprises an allegory — a *modus operandi*, to borrow a term from criminology — for the way modern science works.

My version of this story begins in May 1985. It was less than a great day for science. *Nature* magazine reported that the British Antarctica Survey at Hayley's Bay had discovered that an enormous hole had formed in the ozone layer over the South Pole, allowing dangerous ultraviolet radiation to reach the earth. These billion-dollar scientists admitted, however, that they'd recorded similar readings for the seven previous, consecutive years, and simply discarded the data because what the results told them was theoretically impossible. Their readings, the BAS scientists had decided, were wrong, imperfect measurements produced by flawed instruments. Miscalibration. Like bad carpenters, they blamed their tools.

Spurred by the report in *Nature*, the American scientists in charge of NASA's hundred-million-dollar Nimbus 4 and Nimbus 7 satellite program decided to recheck their stored computer data. The two Nimbus satellites took 250,000 or so atmospheric readings per day. NASA's computers had been programmed to render these comprehensible to the human mind: since ozone readings below a certain level were theoretically impossible, the computers had been programmed to disregard them as errors. As it turned out, seven years of previously discarded Nimbus readings were more than sufficient for NASA computers to draw a detailed map of the mysterious hole. And the Nimbus data indicated something else: The hole was growing bigger every year.

It's important to recall the context of these horrific omissions. A hypothesis for how chlorofluorocarbons in aerosolized cans and air conditioners might destroy the ozone layer was first announced in 1973 by two highly eminent chemists. That story was front-page news in the years following, stirring more concern and effecting more change among more individuals than any other aspect of the then-emerging environmental movement. The citizenry sent more letters to Congress over concern about aerosolized cans than any other issue since Vietnam. Retail sales of aerosol sprays plummeted.

Confronted with such vehement protests, the American government dilly-dallied and created the illusion of action by spending more than a hundred million dollars on research sponsored by agencies ranging from the newly formed Environmental Protection Agency to the Food and Drug Administration, NASA, and the Consumer Product Safety Commission. However, Uncle Sam issued not a single regulation until 1978, and only after a class-action suit was filed against the EPA by the Natural Resources Defense Council. Certain aerosol sprays were banned, and more studies were commissioned, sponsored by the President's Council on Environmental Quality and by the Federal Council for Science and Technology, with the involvement of seven cabinet departments, five government agencies, and echelons of civil servants. Laws against profoundly polluting chlorofluorocarbons were passed by the legislatures of Oregon and New York. The House Subcommittee on Anti-trust and Restraint of Trade Activities and the National Oceanic and Atmospheric Administration studied the problem, along with the Department of Transportation's Climatic Impact Assessment Program. The World Meteorological Organization supplied data to dozens of countries with departments, commissions, agencies, inquiries, and debate, among them the Committee on Impacts of Stratospheric Changes of the American Academy of Sciences. The AAS issued four official reports, each more dire than the last. Measurements in the Northern Hemisphere began to indicate ozone depletion over the North Pole as well.

The response of industries was obstructive; these vested interests resorted to the shield of the notion of the scientific method — the incantatory proclamation "Show us the data." Du Pont promised the government a research program and promptly began to develop new technology to build "the world's largest yo-yo" — a satellite on a string tied to the earth that would take sophisticated measurements of atmospheric ozone. It never got off the ground, but Du Pont managed to stall everyone for three more years in the late 1970s. And just as it was until recently with cigarette manufacturers facing lawsuits claiming that their products caused cancer, the scientific evidence did not satisfy big business. Industry would react to nothing less than a smoking gun.

Meanwhile, over Antarctica, the growing hole in the ozone layer was dutifully recorded by taxpayer-financed computers and scientists who tossed out the data because the results were "theoretically impossible."

It would be incorrect to call this an incident of scientific indifference, because indifference requires an object to ignore; the BAS and Nimbus scientists lived in an ivory tower of abstraction that made objective reality invisible. A scientist invents a hypothesis to explain events he has seen unfold empirically. He designs experiments to test the hypothesis. If the hypothesis has consistent predictive value — it predicts the results or data of the experiments — then it becomes a theory. The sine qua non of the scientist is objective data, because that is what can transform an idea from a hypothesis into a theory. This process of experimentation is known as the scientific method. In public discourse, however, the distinction between hypothesis and theory is invariably omitted. A hypothesis is nothing more than supposition — a shrewd guess. Yet through semantic sloppiness, speculation is sanctified as theory, and the public is left with no linguistic method to distinguish between the two. Obversely, when *theory* is used pejoratively, the speaker is often referring to what is, in fact, hypothesis — or speculation. Thus the scientific method is transformed from a sword of inquiry to a cynical shield for moral, bureaucratic, and industrial entities that are addicted to the status quo.

In a decade that manifested immense public concern for the integrity of the planet's ozone layer, civilization entrusted its safety to British and American meteorologists. That trust was egregiously betrayed. The scientists designed a system of data collection that safeguarded a theory about ozone levels that was wrong, even in the face of controversy, public discourse, and objective data recorded by hundred-million-dollar instruments.

The ozone story is also the modus operandi of AIDS research, ethics, and treatment. From the emergence of the epidemic in 1981 straight into the cheery age of protease inhibitors, people struggling to stay alive have been fighting a pitched battle against those researchers who insist that science must be pure, withdrawn, detached from causes of the heart, and unfettered by the tedium of the patient's concerns or mortality. In a system of scientific solipsism, responsibility to the public and the individual does not exist; only the scientist has value, wielding the scientific method — idea, hypothesis, theory — with statistics, averages, medians, bell curves. Even death is euphemized as a "clinical endpoint," helpfully divorcing a scientist's work from the most elemental human sympathy. Perhaps the only equivalent is in the military, which revels in code words for killing.

Scientists make up a modern version of a priestly caste, and with that status are bestowed the prerogatives of the shaman: mythmaking; prophecy; infallibility. The myth was the spirit of dauntedness that researchers brought to studying acquired immune deficiency syndrome, in spite of the fact that other viral diseases like smallpox and polio had been conquered through vaccines, and despite the existence of treatments for hepatitis and herpes — both viral diseases. Once the cause of AIDS was discovered, the prophecy seemed to follow as the night the day — that everyone

infected with HIV would eventually die from AIDS. Such speculation, which ignored valuable data to the contrary, was parroted by
boilerplates in virtually all the press coverage well into the 1990s,
when scientific and media powers first deigned to note the existence of a significant number of HIV-positive "non-progressors"
whose immune systems sustained little or no damage years after
infection. This conjecture became the public's tenet of faith, and,
perhaps second only to the deaths of friends and lovers, it engendered despair. It certainly made it harder for the people living at
HIV Ground Zero.

After moving to Tucson from the infectiously activist environment of New York, I encountered more despair among HIV-
positive men in Arizona than I ever had in the darkest and most
terrifying days of the epidemic. It was not that the men I met in
Tucson were sicker, or that they were treated by less-informed doctors with less up-to-date treatments (although people with AIDS
even in the big cities are far too often subject to substandard care
and previous-wave medications and therapies by doctors who remain ignorant of new treatments or the best combinations of drugs
to combat the virus). What was most afflicting my new friends in
Tucson was despondency. They lagged a few years behind their
New York and San Francisco counterparts in one deathly way:
they had entirely bought into the prevailing medical notions that
they would die soon. At best they were swallowing their pills and
eating their macrobiotic cabbage in an effort to stave off death. No
one in their lives — no medical authority, no newspaper, no organization of HIV-positive people — told them they even had a chance.

This did not sit well with me. At my urging, Martin Delaney of
San Francisco's Project Inform came to Tucson. He could offer
these HIV-positive people some information about new treatments
and some promise of progress in treating AIDS. But more than anything else, he could give them some perspective on their disease.
His very presence, as an activist who didn't see death from AIDS as

an acceptable answer, helped these men take their bodies back. He disinhibited their hopes.

Delaney's presence also made real the possibility of medical progress. Although science has been constructed around the idea of a fundamentally random universe, the twentieth-century layman's understanding of discovery is primitive, essentially animist. In the event that science would fail to find treatments or even determine the pathology of HIV infection, scientists have maintained the belief in their infallibility by endowing HIV with abilities that are so mysterious they border on the occult and thus understandably baffle brilliant minds. An almost inanimate tangle of stray RNA has been anthropomorphized into a cunning little demon, and magnified many times by the media that reports on scientific discovery. (A newspaper headline read, "Research Reveals a Frustrating New Skill of the AIDS Virus." *Vogue* magazine noted that "different strains of HIV have widely divergent personalities.") HIV's *mens rea*, or "evil intent," sustains the wishful thinking arising from some of society's most fundamental myths: that pleasure must be paid for; that the wages of sin are death. To deny these equations doesn't just contradict scientific speculation; denying them questions the existence of God.

With both AIDS and the ozone fiasco, hypotheses — mere speculation — were vigorously defended as the holy writ of theory. When objective data argued against theory, it was labeled suspect or dismissed. Void of predictive value yet sanctified by the priestly caste, so-called theory was nothing more than myth. We may have found out the causes of AIDS, but we were not about to let truths of the virus upset the liturgy of scientific inquiry.

When AIDS arrived on American shores, the mismatch between myth and science turned infected people into little more than laboratory fodder. In clinical trials of experimental therapies, scientific ethics devolved to a level unseen since the days of Mengele and Tuskegee, and the appalling Cold War experiments in

which unsuspecting Americans were injected with radioactive liq-
uids. Cliff's human urine, Artie's orgone box, and the incantations
of New Age inner children may well have been ineffective, but
they were benevolent in comparison to what researchers were
doing with official seals of approval.

The interplay between myth, superstition, and the holy "scientific method" underlies the utter failure of researchers to find an
effective treatment — and any truly new antiviral drugs — until four-
teen years into the epidemic; prophecies of doom needed to be fulfilled. For those living with HIV, the scientific method became a
machinery of death.

Nothing shows how gay men were doomed to be doomed better
than the story of the so-called pentamidine wars of the 1980s.

Pneumocystis carinii is a microorganism that adores the warm,
moist interior of the human lung. It is found in the lungs of almost
everyone. Only when the immune system has been seriously im-
paired does it begin to grow unchecked, clogging the delicate tissue
of the alveoli, where the interchange of oxygen to the cells takes
place. The alveoli grow viciously inflamed from fluid buildup, one
by one, until the lungs are turned to liquid. This pneumonia was
rarely a problem in America, mainly affecting transplant patients
who took drugs to suppress their immune systems to avoid organ rejection. Then it became the leading killer of men with AIDS.

It is a horrible death. I have seen it. When the lungs grow en-
gorged with fluid, the patient breathes with a respirator inserted
into his throat. His arms are tied down or he is injected with paralyzing drugs so he won't instinctively rip the respirator out. He lies
there, immobile, until heart failure, which can take several weeks,
his last communications crudely printed notes or the twitches of his
eyelids.

In 1986 American PWAs began to hear reports from Europe that
an English drug, pentamidine, administered in an aerosolized

spray, was showing a result as a prophylactic measure against PCP. Thus began the "pentamidine wars," a major preoccupation of treatment activists in the late 1980s as individuals petitioned American medical powers and, later, as organized activists challenged the entire system of drug approvals.

Since there was no American source for aerosolized pentamidine, gay men imported it from England, at twenty-five dollars a dose. It became the standard monthly therapy in any serious AIDS practice. Suddenly the FDA announced that the drug would have to be tested in seven years of trials; in the face of protest, it backed down, waiving the trials by accepting data from other countries. It licensed pentamidine as an orphan drug to a small Chicago outfit. The owners immediately quadrupled the price to one hundred dollars a dose. PWA buyers' clubs continued importing the more affordable doses from England. At the behest of the American licensees, the FDA tried, unsuccessfully, to stop the buyers' clubs. Innumerable activist hours were wasted in this back-and-forth struggle.

Pentamidine is a story of patients and their doctors being far ahead of the scientific and medical establishment and regulatory agencies. But earlier than all of them, one AIDS doctor had taken an entirely different tack; his patients were truly lucky.

Like every other doctor in the early 1980s dealing with the strange new plague originally called GRID, or Gay Related Immune Deficiency, in 1983, Dr. Joseph Sonnabend in New York had seen man after man in his practice slowly asphyxiate. Weary with the kind of numb grief that affects physicians in epidemics, and feeling very much alone in his exploration, Sonnabend went to the medical library at New York University to see what could be done to halt the deaths. He sat at the computer console that led to the on-line catalog, and beside "Subject" typed in the words "Pneumocystis carinii — treatment."

To his surprise, the screen spewed forth a list of references in scientific journals dating back to the early 1970s. Two old-fashioned and inexpensive sulfa drugs had been used to prevent outbreaks of PCP in immunosuppressed organ-transplant patients. There was no gap in Western knowledge about this: Medical science had known how to *prevent* PCP for more than ten years.

Doctors had been treating PCP patients with sulfa drugs and pentamidine since the beginning of the AIDS epidemic — but only after the patients had gotten sick, at which point it was often too late. Since each outbreak destroys more lung tissue, it's better to prevent PCP in the first place than cure it after an outbreak. Immediately, Sonnabend began prescribing this medicine for his patients as a prophylaxis — to be taken every day. One of his patients, the outspoken AIDS activist Michael Callen, insisted that the primary reason he was alive ten years after his AIDS diagnosis was that he had started on Bactrim in 1983. Most people with AIDS weren't so lucky. And other doctors who had stumbled across the same information chose an entirely different course of action from Dr. Sonnabend's.

In 1984, Dr. Margaret Fischl, who would later be called "the Queen of AZT" for her research with the pharmaceutical giant then called Burroughs-Wellcome, published the results of a short trial she had run in which one group of men received Bactrim prophylaxis and the control group a placebo. At the end of her monograph she quoted as references the decade-old trials that Sonnabend had found in the library. During the run of the trial, twenty-eight men in Fischl's control group died of PCP even though Bactrim could have been used to save their lives.

Dr. Fischl's early Bactrim trial passed the ethical review board at her hospital. Perhaps it was because the modern homosexual and his sexual practices were considered so exotic, so entirely new to the medical establishment, that overly rigorous scientists justified starting medical knowledge at zero. Separated from the general population and ghettoized into "risk groups," people with AIDS became a subspecies of humanity. They were exiled to a kind of alternate universe where the knowledge that sat on the shelves of medical libraries, knowledge that could prolong their lives and give them means for hope, was in the real and humanistic world of patient care somehow nonexistent. But it must be made clear that it was not gay men who created that alternate universe; it was the scientists and those who believed them.

A kind of mass cognitive dissonance existed in the medical community: the myth of plague and punishment foreclosed the fate of people with HIV; therefore, how could there possibly exist information to save their lives? Trapped in their fixed notions of what was allowed by Cartesian science, and dealing with people whose lives they saw as dispensable and alien, scientists who predicted that everyone with HIV infection was "doomed" to die of AIDS were determined that their clairvoyance would come true.

Pentamidine turned out not to be as effective as hoped. Because it was breathed in with a mask and penetrated the lungs through gravity, the upper lobes failed to get adequate doses, and men were having breakthroughs of the pneumonia again. Bactrim could be taken orally, though, and penetrated the entire body. Word about its effectiveness moved through a grapevine of activists and physicians with AIDS practices. Treatment newsletters began recommending dosage levels and suggesting desensitization regimens for those who suffered from the often severe side effects. A second old sulfa drug, dapsone, once used to treat leprosy, was found to be effective for many who were allergic to Bactrim.

By the time the "pentamidine wars" were over and that drug was freely available, it was already second- or third-line therapy, and almost irrelevant to urban gay men living with AIDS in New York City, who had propounded more sophisticated treatments. It was an ambuscade, for years diverting energies and lives. Meanwhile, of course, many people with AIDS died, painfully and hopelessly, because science said they had to.

Gay men in the largest cities had the benefit of activism, information bulletins, and gray market buyers' clubs. Ironically, their having been stigmatized into a "risk group" forced them to take command of their health and seek out their own effective treatment solutions. The result was that some of this critical information also became available to seropositive members of the "general population"— drug users, heterosexual men and women, hemophiliacs, and the so-called innocent victims. In September 1989, newspapers reported that Ryan White, America's most famous poster boy with AIDS, had been admitted to an Indiana hospital with PCP. His doctor had never heard of using Bactrim PCP prophylaxis until Michael Callen read of White's hospitalization in the paper, and phoned him.

It now seems prehistoric, those years before people with AIDS knew how to prevent pneumocystis. Yet no single medication has been more important in extending the length and quality of life — a fifty-year-old medicine that costs a dime a pill. Still, countless scientists ran countless more trials to prove it all over again. The FDA finally made it official, and recommended Bactrim as the first line of defense against PCP. In 1994. That kind of bureaucratic time line creates absurd Catch-22 situations for patients and researchers in a host of clinical trials, in some instances forcing them to transgress the boundaries of medical ethics — getting the drugs into bodies that need them, test results be damned.

The use of AZT became another instance where scientific rigidity and the natural human urge for glib hope combined to cause trauma and death, demonstrating what the virus was telling us from the start — that HIV monotherapy was ultimately deadly. AZT was developed at taxpayer expense as a cancer-fighting agent in the early sixties, but it was never marketed because it was considered too toxic. Burroughs-Wellcome discovered its antiviral activity, patented it for HIV disease, and managed to get FDA approval almost overnight. To people with AIDS, it seemed like the first best hope to fight the virus itself. To Burroughs-Wellcome, it promised a profit bonanza. The pharmaceutical company had scientific data from a three-month trial in which PWAs on the drug had lived longer. Critics now claim that the extended life in the first AZT trial reflected the new use of PCP prophylaxis and had nothing to do with the antiviral at all.

Burroughs-Wellcome's marketing of AZT intersected with the cultural longing we all have to stick out our tongues for a magic doctor's magic pill. Trial followed trial, each varying the segment of the population, the ages, genders, level of immune-system destruction. By 1989, the Public Health Service standards, which doctors followed in treating HIV disease, recommended AZT for everyone with fewer than five hundred T cells. For most seropositive people, that's years away from any major decline in health. Gingerly, people began to expect that AIDS would soon be a "manageable disease." This would not be the last time HIV would prematurely be declared "manageable."

People on AZT continued to die. Slowly the great tenuous hope of the late 1980s dissolved into the reality of viral resistance, AIDS progression, and death. Some people remained on the drug for two, three, or four years, under a doctor's guidance, long after their T-cell levels sank and the drug began to poison them. AZT is toxic; indeed, it is a form of chemotherapy that poisons the body. It may further suppress white blood cell production in the bone marrow, cause painful neuropathy in the hands and feet, and atrophy the muscles — "droopy butt syndrome," in the jargon of PWAs. It may also cause liver damage and severe anemia in some people. The perfect colonizing drug, it primed patients to consume ever more pharmaceutical products to counteract its side effects.

Nor did AZT prevent immune-system decline. If someone started taking it when he was healthy, by the time his T-cell level had fallen below fifty and deadly opportunistic infections set in, AZT might already have sapped his body of its resilience to fight disease. A small number of doctors with AIDS practices — such as Bernard Bihari in New York — discouraged their patients from using the drug. Dr. Bihari found it extremely useful in treating dementia, clearing it up in a matter of days — except when someone had been on AZT too long. Then Bihari could do nothing. He preferred to keep it in his armamentarium for late-stage illness, but he prescribed it if his patient demanded it.

European doctors began telling their patients that they had a choice: AZT might slow down the progression to AIDS a little, but when they did get sick, they'd die faster; if they elected not to take AZT, opportunistic infections might occur sooner, but the patient would likely live longer. When Michael Callen published a book surveying the lifestyles of long-term survivors, he found they had only one thing in common: none had taken AZT, himself included.

None of this became official, however, until the results of the Concord Study were released at the international AIDS conference in Berlin, in 1993. That trial indicated that AZT, when taken by HIV-positive individuals with high T-cell counts and no symptoms of disease, conferred no survival benefit whatsoever. When a preview of the data was released in March, American scientists pooh-poohed it, pointing out that the trial design had to be carefully studied for possible flaws. "There is no reason to change any treatment," Daniel Hoth, a director of the government's AIDS research program, told the Associated Press. When the final report was issued in Berlin in June, chagrined doctors could only admit that the trial design looked good after all. It had a placebo wing and large numbers of patients, and it had lasted for three years. A study in Germany indicated that the longer someone took AZT, the *shorter* his expectation of life. Researchers were still so resistant to what their own rigid standards considered objective truth that they spent two more years trying to refute what the Concord Study clearly indicated. In 1995, more headlines rolled in, such as these in the New York Times: "AZT Won't Help Much, Study Suggests"; "Children's AIDS Study Finds AZT Ineffective"; "Early HIV Treatment Doesn't Prolong Survival, Study Finds"; "Early Use of AIDS Drug Is Termed Not Effective." The result was even less promise for survival among people with AIDS, who had grown accustomed by then to being told the truth too late to help them, and who found less reason to hope than ever.

The implications were far more horrifying than the countless ongoing deaths despite the availability of an overly toxic, mediocre antiviral. For eight years, the leadership at the National Institutes of Health steered 80 *percent* of federal funds for testing AIDS drugs into trials for AZT and other nucleoside analogues — a class of drugs that works, when it does work, either immediately after HIV infection, or in concert with more powerful and innovative drugs that until recently have received far less attention than the panacea of AZT and its toxic cousins.

Now, of course, no AIDS doctor worth her salt would prescribe AZT alone, because the benefits of combination or "cocktail" therapies are so evident. Martin Delaney of Project Inform suggests that, given what doctors and patients know about antiviral therapy today, AZT monotherapy should be considered unethical — tantamount to withholding treatment. Objective scientific data had long indicated that cocktail combinations of several antivirals were far more effective — yet in 1995, as protease inhibitor trials opened up across America, each had a placebo-control AZT-monotherapy arm. This sort of dissonance in the landscape of death was manifested in words shouted at researchers by an AIDS activist in Berlin, when after seven years of AZT the results of the Concord Study confirmed the worst: "You staked your career on it! I staked my life!"

The machinery of death has many guises. Part of the problem is undoubtedly *Homo institutus*. The person skilled at rising through institutional and corporate hierarchies is by nature and tactic more reassuring than imaginative, timid rather than risk-taking. Scientific hubris also plays a role, as it has since the story of Daedalus, and the Atlantean *bildungs*-myth of technology without morality. However much they may have witnessed the anguish of AIDS firsthand, however carefully they have listened to reasoned AIDS activists with HIV in their bodies, for these research professionals saving the lives of the infected was not the point. Remote from the reality of diseased bodies, the governmental-scientific complex grew addicted to its method.

Instead the seropositive were offered myth: science is helpless; the virus, all-powerful. Even today with news of a fresh vaccine trial, or progress in gene therapy, or the advent of some new treatment beyond today's received wisdom of protease inhibitors, the announcement must always end with a ritual dance of words masked as sagacity and prudence: "It will be years before this translates into treatment, if at all." The dance concludes with the announcement of continuing research, conducted in the utmost interest of humankind.

"We have never cured a viral illness" is the litany mouthed by scientists to excuse their failures. Such mendacity occludes an obvious fact that might, in another world or another time, be another basis for hope: our own extraordinary human bodies cure and control viral illnesses all the time.

For a person living with HIV, treatment decision-making involves reasoning and intuition more than quantities and specifics of knowledge. No system of education is in place to teach the rubric of wellness to individuals. Quite the opposite. Good patients do what their doctors tell them.

In terms rather Whitmanesque, I refer to my own strategy as "listening to the body." My physician is a partner in management, not an authority on high. Sometimes this approach is very difficult for doctors, particularly those more priestly professionals who entered the profession to enjoy their status as givers of wisdom and protocols. Yet the best doctors have the curiosity and heart to interact with their patients. Marcus Conant, a doctor in San Francisco, said in 1994, "As a doctor who's cared for AIDS patients since 1981, I'm not too arrogant to admit that most of what I've learned about AIDS has been from my patients."

Early in HIV disease, many changes can occur in a person's body. For everyone it can be different: more-virulent herpes outbreaks, incredible dandruff, white fungus under toenails, red patches on the face, jock itch that will not go away. These are the "soft signs" of HIV infection, indications of an immune system in decline. In allopathic medicine, we are taught to see these as symptoms to be suppressed, and we have all the necessary drugs to do that: acyclovir, cortisone, fluconazole, lotrisone. Allopathic medicine tells us that these "little things" should be battled aggressively, because each represents further strain on an immune system already embattled with HIV.

I came to understand, however, that my body was speaking to me through such soft signs. I recognized this even before I fully acknowledged to myself that I was seropositive. HIV causes change in the chemical mixture that propels life, and the resulting imbalances became apparent in various ways on the surface of the skin.

I discovered by accident how to listen to my body. I had been "plagued," as the allopaths would put it, by seborrheic dermatitis — dandruff from hell. I began using a dark, musky-smelling shampoo that listed coal tar as an ingredient. When I asked my physician why it had coal tar, he answered, "Because it contains zinc. And zinc kills the little microorganisms that cause the dandruff." He mentioned that another leading brand of dandruff shampoo contained selenium. I had already learned enough about HIV disease to know that seropositive people often have low levels of zinc and selenium. The next day I bought zinc supplements. That was six years ago, and the dermatitis disappeared — except when I became neglectful and stopped taking supplements or used a different kind of shampoo for a while. It was an object lesson in how to approach a chronic viral infection.

Later, I became aware of a quiet whispering noise periodically in my right ear. Sometimes it was accompanied by a half-second swoon, as if my balance mechanism, the bones behind the ear, had bleeped off, then on. I discovered that tinnitus, a ringing in the ear, is a possible sign of vitamin B12 deficiency. This is another common problem in HIV infection, and sometimes it can be so serious it can lead to malnutrition, hospitalization, and death. Unfortunately, B12 is not well absorbed when taken by mouth; most is digested and excreted. At my request, my physician wrote a prescription for cyanocobalamin, pharmaceutical B12, and his nurse taught me how to inject myself weekly with a thousand milligrams. Each injection costs about a dollar, and the tinnitus disappeared.

Dandruff and a little noise in the ear are hardly major problems on the scale of what many people with HIV can face. But to me those little signs were indications of what essential nutrients my body lacked as a result of my infection. Since those early days, I have followed a kind of "keep plugging the dike" strategy: by listening to my body and keeping informed, I try to restore my body's amino acids, hormones, cytokines, and nutrients to their normal levels, hoping that when I do so there is a cascade of benefit through my body. The records of my blood indicate that even as I must work to maintain an effective number of T cells, I have drastically forestalled the decline of my immune system and kept my viral burden relatively low.

Listening to the body can encourage me. If I go for a year without athlete's foot, my body is telling me I can still fight disease; when a scab forms on a wound, I know I can heal quickly; when my stool floats, friendly bacteria are alive in my bowels; when the volume of my ejaculate is abundant, my DHEA and testosterone levels are in normal ranges.

Long-term survivors share one factor: each has tried many different strategies and stuck with what worked for him. In the wave of orgone therapy, urine therapy, and other alternative treatments that wash over the community, only a few have endured, because they've proved effective for some people, stabilizing their immune systems or minimizing opportunistic infections. Few have been subject to clinical trials in a way that would convince most doctors, but people can manifest a collective common sense that escapes the measurement of science.

Some apparently useful therapies involve the off-label use of FDA-approved pharmaceuticals. Ketotifen, a European asthma drug and powerful anti-inflammatory, might thwart tumor necrosis factor and seems to restore intestinal function, ending diarrhea and allowing the patient to gain weight and absorb medicine; N-acetylcysteine, sold over the counter in Europe for bronchitis, restores glutathione levels, which seem to be depleted in cells with HIV disease. This was finally confirmed in a 1996 study, although activists talked about it for years. Naltrexone, normally used to block heroin addiction, has appeared to stabilize skewed interferon levels when taken in very small doses.

Chinese herbs are commonly used to boost the immune system, and most people taking them report a noticeable improvement in their quality of life because of renewed energy. Free radicals seem to play a strong role in the progression of HIV disease, leading to antioxidation treatment strategies and "neutriceuticals" or vitamin therapy. Acupuncture treatments are considered highly beneficial, along with cardiovascular exercise and stress reduction.

Virtually all of these alternative treatments have been used for decades, if not centuries, and are known to be safe. Because they're in the public domain, they're usually fairly inexpensive. While it is nice that people can afford them, there is no capitalistic incentive for a private company to conduct formal clinical trials to measure their efficacy or most appropriate doses. While some alternative therapies can be toxic, the best ones stave off the immune system's final crash by restoring the body's chemical cascade to something a little closer to normal. This kind of HIV treatment exists at the margins of the mainstream, certainly off the path taken by the great research labs and scientific bureaucracies of government. Such regimens remain far outside the "official" treatments approved by the FDA.

Some doctors, as well as other wellness professionals, are credited with early extraordinary success in stabilizing the health of the majority of patients in their practice. In Washington, D.C., Lark Lands, a former Rand Corporation scientist, employed a "think tank approach" to HIV disease in 1985 — which is what the federal government should have done at the very beginning. She researched existing medical knowledge that could be used to counter the effects of HIV in the body. Within three years, she was able to offer a program of nutrition, supplements, and immunomodulators that was far in advance of its time. In New York, Dr. Bernard Bihari claimed to have stabilized the immune systems of the majority of his patients, in many cases for years, using certain pharmaceuticals off-label as immunomodulators. In San Francisco, Dr. John Kaiser has combined various forms of holistic therapy with his Western medical knowledge. These are a few of a small number of physicians who step beyond the confines of ordinary allopathic practice to keep their patients alive and healthy.

Almost always, standard-issue scientists denigrate claims about alternative therapies. It would be a simple matter to institute studies known as "outcomes research" and "physician profiling" — compiling retrospective data on patients undergoing these treatments and observing their present status. Yet again, orthodox scientists dismiss this kind of research, although drug companies and health maintenance organizations spend millions on outcomes research to determine cost-efficient treatment decisions.

Treatment activists should start working directly with insurers and outcomes studies to develop treatment protocols independently of the slow-moving public health agencies. Thousands of people with HIV who spent thousands on antiviral therapy early in the disease would likely have been far better off with vitamins, acupuncture, and Naltrexone, at far cheaper cost.

It's inordinately difficult for the leaders of the medical-research establishment to admit that, in most instances, the criticisms and proposals of AIDS activists have consistently proved to be wiser than the practices and decisions of agencies and authorities — at least if *wiser* means "life-saving" to people infected with HIV. In 1989, the Treatment and Data Committee of ACT UP announced an initiative called Countdown 18 Months. These treatment activists had realized that HIV does not directly kill humans; opportunistic infections that overwhelm compromised immune systems do. The example of Bactrim and *Pneumocystis carinii* was a case in point. Antiviral research seemed to be going nowhere fast, and the severe limitations of AZT were swiftly becoming apparent. With a list of a dozen of the most serious opportunistic infections in hand, and a parallel column of possible treatments that needed to be studied as quickly as possible, Countdown 18 Months was designed to challenge the authorities to make successful treatments available for those opportunistic infections within an eighteen-month period. The NIH refused to endorse the initiative; its director, Dr. Anthony Fauci, criticized it as impractical, stating that "science can't be rushed." Except, apparently, when it came to developing the atomic bomb, and the government created the Manhattan Project to assemble the best scientists to hasten the objective.

The Treatment and Data Committee achieved only limited success in the eighteen-month period, and the initiative never attained legitimacy in the eyes of those who controlled purse strings and research priorities at taxpayer-funded institutions. Within the decade, however, most of the treatments that were finally current were ones that had been on T&D's 1989 list. From the point of view of a person with AIDS, in a world where HIV antivirals remain costly, toxic, difficult to comply with, and not reliable for all, few other research efforts have improved the quality or length of life more than the treatments now available for the disabling and lethal secondary infections that define AIDS.

Important exceptions remain. *Cryptosporidium*, a protozoan that can pollute drinking water and infects the gut, has been killing people with AIDS since the beginning of the health crisis. Progress in treating the infection has occurred, but it has been slow. People have gone as far as trying veterinary medicines to relieve the debilitating diarrhea. In 1993, the city of Milwaukee suffered an epidemic of crypto infection through the water supply. Some three hundred people died, including almost seventy PWAs. Subsequent research on American water-filtration systems indicates that current public treatment techniques do not eliminate the cysts that cause infection. The Centers for Disease Control and Prevention responded by issuing guidelines warning PWAs not to drink municipal tap water. Those who could afford it installed special carbon filters in their homes, but the danger lurks in ice cubes, water fountains, restaurant glasses, and even bottled water. And peril continues to exist for all those who either don't know the risks or can't buy clean private water. Dr. Charles Sterling, a world expert on *Cryptosporidium* at the University of Arizona, has said that we must still ask such elementary questions as, How much concentration of parasite is needed to infect AIDS patients? and, Over what period of time? Hearing this, a CDC spokesperson shrugged, and said, seventeen years after his agency listed cryptosporidiosis as an opportunistic infection, "We don't have enough data."

With the advent of protease inhibitors, people can choose to believe that AIDS is over, that the big issues have been dealt with and only loose ends remain. Yet a list of research and treatment travesties would still fill books. No one with any political power, anything approaching high profile, or any genuine influence has ever been put in charge of national policy toward AIDS treatment and prevention. Presidential councils come and go; so-called AIDS czars serve in obscurity at the pleasure of presidents who want to keep AIDS activism muffled more than they want to surmount the disease. No group or think tank has been given the official job of drawing up an action plan for research that might actually save the lives of those infected today. The free market will not go where no profit is found. The U.S. Department of Health and Human Services will not authorize federal needle-exchange programs that have been proved to save lives; safer-sex programs are still hamstrung nationwide. Many people cannot afford treatment with the drugs that are in fact available, and hundreds of needy people have been cut off from stingy and short-sighted drug-supply programs in Arizona, Florida, and other states; when state money runs out, so do those states' citizens' antiviral cocktails — leading to new HIV infections resistant to drugs, more costs, and more deaths: an aggravated plague and a plague of shamefulness. Scientists remain quiet in the face of such travesties; they share the shame.

Nothing raised more furor among the caste of scientists than the intrusion of patient activists into the inner sanctums of their conferences, and into federal policy-making. As recently as 1995, the *Bulletin for Experimental Treatments for AIDS* used the phrase "collegial atmosphere" as a circumspect way to inform researchers of conferences where treatment activists would not be present. To scientists who will determine their fate, the patients' absence is the advertised draw.

The media are of no help whatsoever. When treatment activists went to confer with the FDA in 1994 about new drug-authorization strategies, the press gloatingly presented their complaints as sheepish mea culpas from radical AIDS patients who had realized that their desperate and puerile demands for faster access to pharmaceutical drugs should yield to the slow and sage procedures of pure science. An article in *Barron's* entitled "Rushing to Judgment" contained such lines as "In a turnabout . . ." and "Four years later, the tune has changed." The real story was substantially different. Despite accelerated approval for certain antivirals, drug companies had quietly dropped plans for further trials that the FDA had requested as a condition of approval. The data that existed were almost useless for doctors and patients to decide how to use the drugs in question properly. Buried in the article was the statement that everyone supported speedy approval of useful new drugs, and that fault lay with dishonest pharmaceutical companies and a regulatory agency that neglected to fulfill its mandate.

With science lacking morality, the stakes have never been as high, because the products of science have never had more potential for destruction. Perhaps it is time for our society to label and punish a new kind of crime, one for which our civilization has not yet evolved a name: scientific misconduct that results in the loss of life; dereliction of scientific duty that harms the public interest.

The scientists responsible for the fiasco of missed data concerning disappearing atmospheric ozone have gone on in their careers. Meanwhile, children in New Zealand and Tierra Del Fuego wear sunglasses, while herds of sheep develop cataracts, and fish have cancer. Among the major figures of early AIDS research, Dr. Margaret Fischl has since been in charge of drawing up national treatment guidelines for AIDS; Dr. Robert Gallo, whose reported improprieties include malfeasance in the discovery of HIV, not to mention highly disputed lab data for a KS treatment that other labs have been unable to replicate, has left the NIH to build his own prestigious lab with government financing; Dr. Ellen Cooper, who many believe became the primary obstructionist for access to new drugs when she was at the FDA in the 1980s, was later responsible for determining clinical research priorities at the American Foundation for AIDS Research. For people with AIDS there has been little justice; for these early scientists, there has been no justice either.

The invention of a category of scientific crime will not come easily. When a New York doctor mistakenly used an elderly woman's kidney dialysis tube to feed her, the patient died and he became the first doctor in New York State subjected to criminal charges for his negligence. He was convicted not for his medical mistake but for trying to cover it up. The American Medical Association was outraged. "Mistakes of judgment should not be liable to criminal prosecution," stated Dr. James Todd, a vice president of the AMA, claiming for doctors an exemption for the sort of criminal negligence that every ordinary layperson bears. A professional-conduct board refused to punish the New York doctor.

Even before the AIDS crisis, many gay men regarded science and medicine as a priestly sham, since as homosexuals they had already been labeled everything from "mentally depraved" to victims of arrested emotional development, and all kinds of doctors, not just psychiatrists, were complicit in the oppression of homosexuals, even when scientific and medical evidence pointed straight at their normality. As early as 1982, activist Michael Lynch, writing in the *Body Politic*, warned that in confronting AIDS, "we need a much fuller picture of the political terrain among researchers." Like Toto in *The Wizard of Oz*, gay activists lifted the curtain on the Emerald City and saw not a wizard, but a Rube Goldberg contraption, with lots of bells, whistles, steam jets, and sparks.

Gay men were practiced at refusing to believe the narratives a culture handed out. They peered skeptically at received truths and refused to accept a sentence of doom as ukase. It was clear that the same institutions that had defined homosexual behavior for two millennia were now marginalizing homosexual men and minimizing their needs and the truths of their own bodies. These were the choices gay men saw before them: passive acceptance of treatment, or forcefully managing one's own care; health care providers as authority figures, or as partners; a belief that all the infected must die, or an effort to create new narratives for the altered situation. These dichotomies were a direct result of the politics of a political movement that, before all else, demanded autonomy for the individual in decisions about his body. And by extension, the choices gay men made included access to the forums of scientists, input on research priorities, and participation in trial design.

Critic Douglas Crimp has pointed out a relationship between sexual play among men in the 1970s and their ability to adapt quickly to safer-sex practices a few years later. In his essay "How to Have Promiscuity in an Epidemic," first published in 1987 in *October* magazine, Crimp claimed that the experience gay men had in opening their bodies to pleasure — including the ingestion of recreational drugs — meant that swallowing pills, painting solutions on the skin, and using herbal enemas were not completely alien to them. While drug use would become a major contributing factor to the spread of HIV, and thus a significant moral and epidemiological problem, the idea that the body's responses should be open to exploration was a radical one that would benefit them in reacting to the epidemic. Grafted onto existing community institutions, a kind of "parallel government" was created — from Gay Men's Health Crisis to Martin Delaney's Project Inform — to provide social services, to expand access to treatment options, and even to research new drugs.

After years of street activism, by the end of the 1980s mechanisms were being established to facilitate communication between two of the fronts: clinical practice, and the ivory tower of America's research centers. Gay men's response to the AIDS crisis has radically altered the relationship between patient and doctor, researcher and community, for everyone. In the years since, activists for breast cancer, Alzheimer's, and mental illness have all adopted positions that originated in AIDS activism. It is one gift that people with AIDS and their allies have given to North Americans. Those activists in the fight against other diseases who are challenging so-called AIDS exceptionalism — the idea that AIDS needs special attention from researchers and specific government support — and are maintaining that AIDS should be tracked and reported like other, arguably less stigmatizing sexually transmitted diseases must remember that they would not even have a voice or plan of action were it not for the AIDS combatants whose piece of the pie they would like to pare.

For many years, treatment activists have called for a modern Manhattan Project to focus research in the same way that America developed the atomic bomb. Despite the track record treatment activists had racked up, the sense of urgency that materialized in the 1980s ebbed through 1995 to what medical activist John James calls "a well-developed ideology of fatalism" that undermined it. With the advent of protease inhibitors, that fatalism abruptly converted into a thoughtless optimism. Other virulent diseases will not die even if AIDS does. Alien microbes emerging in different spots on the planet hint that AIDS may be only the beginning of what could descend upon us. Yet there is no consideration of how to establish an emergency response system that would attempt to develop effective treatments immediately, instead of fifteen to twenty years later. Then again, of course, maybe the next AIDS will strike important people who will demand the treatment they are convinced they deserve. Maybe the next risk groups will be United States senators. Or government doctors.

But of course AIDS is over. That's what the media are telling us, content as they are to trumpet the newest and most tantalizing myth around the AIDS pandemic, one that eerily reprises what we first heard whispered around AZT years earlier. We are told that thanks to the existence of protease inhibitors and the cocktail they are part of, AIDS is not just a manageable disease but a disappearing one. It is a myth we ache to embrace. And it is our most dangerous hope.

Nearly fifteen years after the epidemic began, a treatment finally seemed to thwart the progress of HIV through the human bloodstream. Or, to put it more accurately: limited evidence suggests that among many North American middle-class people, at least those who have insurance, and who can comply with the regimen of thirteen to fifty-six pills a day (counting medications people might take to combat opportunistic infections) to keep from spawning a drug-resistant mutation of HIV — some of which pills must be taken on an empty stomach, some requiring refrigeration, some administered with food — and who never get sick with the flu or other digestive disorder that eliminates the undigested drug from their body and thus makes them grow resistant in as little as one missed dose, who have no drug- or alcohol-dependency issues that keep them from adhering precisely to the regimen, who have not been AIDS antiviral pioneers and built up resistance to other drugs that keep protease drugs or nucleoside analogue drugs from working at all, and who have not been infected by people whose HIV is already drug-resistant, and who are *lucky* — among *those* people, the cocktail works just fine. Many people can excuse themselves from inclusion in any one of those dependent clauses. How many will remain exempt in the future?

Just as news of the worth of pentamidine spread through the AIDS community in the 1980s, and just as patients themselves first knew the limitations of AZT, so people with AIDS are the ones who know both the hopes and the hazards of protease inhibitors. We loved the hopes first of all; long bereft, we were again romanced by promise. Until the summer of 1995, AIDS treatment seemed mostly a matter of retarding the virus and prolonging a life that would inevitably be cut short. The initial flood of success and promise caused by AIDS activism had mostly evaporated. The leaders of the fight were themselves dead or dying: Michael Callen, Iris de la Cruz, Tom Cunningham, Daniel Sotomeyer, Robert Rafsky, Vito Russo. Many gay men and lesbians and their allies had moved on to other, sexier and clean-cut causes. HIV infection was rumored to be rising once again among the young, gay and straight, as the wartime regimen of safer sex seemed impossibly deathly, and HIV moved more vehemently into other less white, less gay populations who possessed even less political and social power to marshal against it.

In the pervading gloom, when everything looked lost for this generation, it was hard to believe we had accomplished anything. In fact, we had won, at great cost, a single great victory, the right to take value in our own bodies and to try to take command of their fates. It was an accomplishment echoing the highest goals of gay liberation, venerating the body in sickness and in health. But it was not a cure for AIDS.

So with a combination of urgency and disbelief we swallowed the antiviral cocktail. We traded among ourselves, and the media hurried to provide, stories of miracles, of men and women who had been next to dead and yet rose and walked and even went back to work — or who asked themselves the great question that most of us as individuals and as patients have barely begun to consider: What now?

But we knew the harder truths about the cocktail as well. We knew how hard it was to take, how hard to tolerate. We knew that the rigors of safer-sex rules seem like motherly suggestions compared to the enforced regimen of swallowing pills every fucking day for the rest of your life. And for every two people whose T-cell levels soared and whose viral load was undetectable, we knew one who spent days vomiting, going through the pharmacopoeia of protease inhibitors as if they were different brands of emetics. We knew how hard the drugs were to take, how hard it was to swallow Crixivan on an empty stomach exactly every eight hours when you also were struggling to keep from wasting. We saw people for whom the drugs worked, but whose cholesterol shot up to two thousand. We witnessed others lose their body fat, the veins of their limbs pulsing against skin thin as silk. Still others we saw develop pads of fat, "buffalo humps" that made them look like premature dowagers. We know more and more people whose T-cell levels escalate — only, for no good reason, to plummet again abruptly even as their viral loads rocket upward. We've all feared disaster that could strike if late at night someone mugged you for your backpack, the backpack with all your antivirals inside, and no all-night pharmacy would give you more without a prescription, and you went without.

One cruel irony of the antiviral cocktail is just now appearing: the longer you have fought the good fight, the less likely you are to thrive on the new drugs. Stephen Gendin, writing in *POZ* magazine in 1998, has said that none of the drugs have worked for him; the reason, he thinks, is that when he found out he was HIV-positive in the mid-1980s he adopted a hit-hard, hit-early strategy that may have backfired, leading him to build up resistance to the new cocktail. While even antiviral veterans can do well on the new regimen, others whose genotype testing tells them they are resistant to AZT and other nucleoside analogues often do less well. In comparison to those who are drug naive or recently infected — at least those whose dose of fresh virus has not come from someone on the cocktail, and who thus do not grow instantly resistant to protease inhibitors — the activist veterans of the antiviral battles do not always reap the results of the harvest they helped to seed.

We all know the social side effects of the antiviral cocktail: the relapse of the American public into caring less about HIV; the relapse into unsafe sex by a younger generation gay and straight who see the toxic cocktail as the equivalent of a morning-after pill or at worst a dollop of herpes; the drying up of government funding and private philanthropy, especially for AIDS care centers and therapies, as the AIDS population sinks out of sight, commandeering its numbers more from an oppressed underclass and less from prosperous and vocal middle-class gay men. But there are other, humanist side effects as well, which over the long term might be just as pernicious. For what is arising around a disease known for spurring others to build barriers and walls is yet another kind of apartheid —

between past and present, AIDS and post-AIDS, death and what just might be life.

Possessed of our cocktails, weary, eager to be released from the past, we are like emigrants sailing to a new country, already practicing the new language even as we forget the vocabulary of the old, oppressive homeland. We fervently tell ourselves we are not like those dead people with AIDS. We're survivors. This interior conversation may grow louder if in convenient forgetfulness we decide we have nothing new to learn from the battles of our forerunners — nothing to learn about the struggle for health care or against bureaucracy, nothing about the drama of taking charge of our physical selves. Enamored of our bodies laden with their undetectable viral load, we might not look with curiosity or reverence at those dead ones whose example has allowed us command of our bodies. Are those who forget the past doomed to die from it?

In a large American city with a well-defined gay community, imagine a narrow door in a brick wall, around the corner from a bar and on a busy street. Three days a week from 10 A.M. to 3 P.M., people are going in and out, a little furtively perhaps. Many of them are men, in haircuts and outfits recognizable as being from the gay ghetto, and some have the sunken cheeks and tannined skins of the contemporary person living with AIDS.

Inside the door, some people flash membership cards, or for out-of-towners an empty container of Viracept with their name on it will do — anything to prove that they have AIDS. Once past the door guard, they face a long, narrow staircase, and at the top another formidable fire door. The moment it swings open, everything changes.

First, there is noise — the friendly, animated human gabbing of a huge cocktail party. Through a haze of smoke, pungent with the scent of burning herb, a sea of couches and sofas, chesterfields and davenports, divans and hassocks, all of Goodwill vintage, stretches across two thousand square feet of loft space. They're arranged into dozens of small, conversational areas around coffee tables of every shape and period.

A giant rainbow flag, sixty feet long and thirty feet wide, covers the entire ceiling. The walls are hung haphazardly with AIDS activist posters and spider plants. And most of all, the room is jammed with people, men and women, black, white, Latino, from teenagers to the white-haired elderly. Most of them have HIV or AIDS. Some have wasted down to the size of skeletons. Others are apparently healthy, doing well on their antiviral cocktails or alternative therapies. Some of them are huddled over small wood trays balanced on their laps, their fingers busy. Everyone is either smoking, passing, or rolling a marijuana joint.

This is the headquarters of the Medical Marijuana for People with AIDS Buyers' Club, and its existence is an open secret in the city. Marijuana has proven medical benefits in stimulating appetite and controlling nausea, both of which are major quality-of-life issues in HIV disease. Although the government has tried to steer people toward Marinol, an expensive, FDA-approved pharmaceutical form of cannabis, plain old marijuana is more accessible to people who lack money to pay for physicians and prescriptions, and is often more easily manageable in terms of dosage. Several grades of marijuana are available at a long counter on one side, where the clerks hold out trays of different quality and price. Cannabinoids are inactive until heated through smoking or baking. For those who want to avoid inhaling smoke, an arresting selection of brownies, cookies, and muffins is available.

The buyers' club was founded by a long-time community activist and advocate for the legalization of marijuana. With AIDS, the need became more urgent. Like all the other therapies used to maintain the length and quality of their lives, the fraternity of people living with AIDS didn't wait. They don't have time. Even against death, revolution can be joyful.

[4]

Disposal

A DEATH AND
LIFE IN AMSTERDAM

WAS SUMMONED from New York by a transatlantic call.
"I've decided to quit."
"How — ?"
"It's legal here in Amsterdam. My doctor will come to the house. I want you to be with me. And everything's all right. It really is."

A week later I stepped from Schiphol airport terminal into the gray dawn of Holland, greeted by a cold, damp wind off the North Sea. A car pulled to the curb, and when I saw Hans at the wheel, for just a moment the reason for my visit was forgotten, replaced by the simple joy of seeing him again. But as I climbed inside it was back, the stark, alien presence of the virus, in the opalescent sheen of the skin that wrapped his emaciated body, his handsome face turned lupine and long of tooth.

I averted my gaze and stared through the windshield. He drove onto the expressway leading to Amsterdam, the tulip fields of Holland stretching to the horizon in ribbons of color. Then I reminded myself that those hazel eyes were still the ones that had gazed at me across a table in a bar ten years earlier.

I was drifting across the face of Europe, and my sojourns took me to the ancient, cobbled streets of Amsterdam, a city of gabled houses and red tile roofs. It seemed that all the flotsam and jetsam of the world washed up in Amsterdam, not for any particular reason, but because it was a beach, and exotic enough. In the taverns and the hashish cafés, there were aging hippies from the sixties, stranded by the war in Afghanistan, young Americans out of high school and looking for kicks, gay men exploring the sexual underworld, exiles and expatriates in search of Isherwood, or oblivion.

In the latest hours of night back then, I haunted an after-hours bar called the Viking Club, where, after I knocked, a door guard peered through a tiny circular window in the door. I passed directly through the lower bar and dance floor, and ascended steep Dutch steps to the topmost room, where big rubber boots were suspended from the ceiling like the feet of drowned men bobbing in water. A thick doorway led into a room in the next building. Through a pungent haze of smoke from hash and tobacco, young men played pool, or hunched over chessboards at tables along the back of the room.

One night, around 4 A.M., just as I leaned across a crowded table to light my cigarette from a candle, a hand touched my arm and I heard a lightly accented voice: "If you do that, a sailor drowns at sea." I turned and saw a blond man, tall and thin, with mocking eyes and a steady smile.

"Whenever someone lights a cigarette from a candle," he explained, "a sailor drowns at sea."

I raised my brows skeptically at a superstition that was alien to me, but held my cigarette aloft. "Then you should give me a light."

By some decree of chemistry or destiny or luck, the world stopped its rotation. We sat and talked until the room was empty, and outside the sun rose above the red tile roofs of Amsterdam. A few days later, Hans led me to his home. He lived in a garret he had renovated under the roof of an old house, where the eaves formed an interior like an A-frame, with a loft bed built in the apex. Night after night, we stumbled home from the Viking Club, climbed the ladder to his bed, and fell asleep to sunrise and the song of waking birds.

Hans was a *krakker*, a squatter, and like hundreds of formerly vacant buildings across the city, his dwelling on Frederikstraat was a *krakhuis*, an occupied house. If the authorities tried to evict squatters from one building, thousands would gather to defend it, often in confrontations that became pitched battles between the police and protesters. These radical politics fascinated me, as did so much in this little, liberal society, where prostitutes advertised their wares behind plate glass windows in the red-light district, hash was available over the counter in certain cafés, municipal swimming pools reserved one night a week for nudists, and even anarchists were given a weekly allotment of television broadcast time.

"Everyone has a turn," Hans explained. He became my guide through the wonders of a tolerant country that, with free health care, guaranteed annual incomes, cheap public transportation, and government-built housing for the middle classes, seemed to verge sometimes on social democratic utopia.

"Be careful what you think," Hans warned once. "Sometimes these liberal ideas are just a way for the government to control people even more." *Dutch disease*, he explained, was the term that critics used for the government's relentless efforts to regulate all aspects of human behavior.

The damp, cold days of winter gave way to spring and flowers, and with them, the date of my airplane ticket home. That morning, we left the loft bed in the garret at Frederikstraat and drove to Schiphol airport. In the midst of crowds swirling through the terminal, we kissed and laughed, and refused to say goodbye.

Ten years later, Hans would be my guide through yet another

intimacy of Dutch life: legal euthanasia, the role of widow, and rituals for the dead.

Hans drove from Schiphol to a highway restaurant that straddled the freeway like an overpass. It was almost deserted in the early-morning hour, and we took our coffees to a table by the window. Below us, the highway was thick with traffic, workers streaming south to jobs in Amsterdam, the headlights of their cars gliding under the window and out of sight beneath our feet.

With the advent of AIDS among gay men — a segment of Dutch society that was both well-educated and demanding of its rights — doctor-assisted euthanasia moved to the forefront on the Dutch agenda. What the government could not effectively forbid it decided it must regulate. In 1988 a group of doctors and judges from the Dutch high court developed a protocol that requires the patient with a life expectancy of six months or less to express in writing his or her wishes to die, and to be examined by two doctors at least two days before the event. After the death, the papers are forwarded to a panel of judges in The Hague. If all requirements of the protocol are met, the law does not prosecute.

Hans told me his arrangements. It would happen in one week, if all went according to plan. His friend Marco would take care of the legal details, the will, the funeral arrangements. The doctor would come right to the apartment.

"And how will it be done?" I asked reluctantly.

"A drink," he said.

I heaved a sigh of relief. Watching Hans gulp down handfuls of pills seemed sordid and desperate. Suicide machines are macabre. And, at least in America, lethal injections have all the appeal of a southern death chamber.

"Drinking something lends it a certain classical nobility," I said, in a feeble attempt at humor. "Like Socrates."

"That's why I like it too," Hans smiled. "And he was one of us. Like a role model." He explained the ritual he had planned. Marco and I were to come at six in the evening. We would have an hour together, before the doctor arrived. Hans had a special glass he was going to use, one he'd saved from a drinking bout as a young man in Sweden. When he went into his bedroom to drink the liquid, he wanted to be alone.

"Before I made this decision I had no energy and I was very depressed. But after I decided this was what I wanted to do, all my spirits came back," Hans smiled. "I'm glad we have this choice in our country."

It was in such contrast to the limited choices foisted upon the terminally ill in America. I told him of men with AIDS I knew who had kept their plans a deathly secret, sending all their friends away so they wouldn't be charged with murder. And the methods were gruesome. Handfuls of pills. Guns in the mouth. Throwing themselves from the Golden Gate Bridge, or the heights of high buildings, tied to their lovers by cords from the venetian blinds. High buildings were a favorite in New York.

"That's just suicide," said Hans dismissively, standing to leave.

I looked at him curiously.

"Let's go for a drive," he said. "I want to buy hyacinths."

Although I was fatigued and cranky from my transatlantic journey, I did not complain, and Hans was quite oblivious to my need for sleep. Already he had entered a different world from the one in which I lived, a world in which, because the appointed hour and method of his death loomed, he was entitled to every whim.

We drove out into the flat, fertile polders of Holland, where swaths of white, crimson, and butter yellow tulips stretched for acres on every side. Stopping at roadside flower stands, Hans, a tall, bony figure, poked his fingers among buckets of blossoms and filled my arms with bouquets. He addressed the farm ladies in rapid

Dutch, always beginning with a joke that made them laugh. It was a habit of his. When he addressed strangers, he made them laugh with a wry and often mocking humor.

He had learned how to be charming after his mother died of cancer when he was six; it had been a way to gain attention from the mothers of his friends while his own mother's photograph hung above the stove like an image of the Madonna. He liked to do things for people, and in some vague, childish, quasi-religious way dedicated his acts of generosity to her. At night, with the lights out in the single bedroom he shared with his two older brothers, the little boy called through the darkness, "Are you still there? Are you smiling?"

He was barely thirteen when he discovered that he could bicycle into Rotterdam and go to the gay saunas. And the sea was in his family's blood. Like his ancestors before him, he wanted to be a sailor; he ran away at sixteen to work in the galleys of freighters plying the cold waters of the Baltic Sea.

In his early twenties he settled in Sweden with a woman and sired a daughter, escaping occasionally across the Baltic to Copenhagen for his secret gay life. Finally he came out, left his wife and daughter, and joined a commune of gay militants that called themselves Red Faggots. Once, these young men stayed up all night drinking from shot glasses, and with the heady exuberance of alcohol and youth vowed that at the age of forty they'd meet again as transvestites in Antwerp. Hans would never live to forty. At thirty-six, he would use the little glass he saved from that evening to hold the poison that ended his life.

In 1978, Hans moved back to Holland, into the attic of the house on Frederikstraat. After I went back to New York, I would return for visits again and again, and each time we fell immediately into the carelessness of our first romantic days. In between we stayed connected through letters and phone calls, a T-shirt arriving in the mail, the arrival of an envoy bearing honey Hans had bought in the Alps. Each of us acquired new boyfriends, new apartments. And as romances do, ours had its crises. Once at least in anger, remembering a strange superstition from the foggy waters of the Baltic Sea, I leaned my cigarette deliberately toward a candle, and lit it from the flame. But later, his heart ravaged by an unrequited love for someone else, Hans sobbed in my arms, "Why do you keep coming back?" and I answered, for the very first time, "Because I love you."

Never cursed by ambition, and with a love of travel, Hans worked for men who raced homing pigeons, driving trucks loaded with thousands of the birds from Holland to the south of France. On broad, wet plains north of Marseilles they were released. The sky was darkened by the ascending multitude, the flapping fury of their sudden freedom like thunder. Then, from the living cloud plunged a gruesome rain, hundreds of broken birds, beaten bloody by the wings of their brethren in the panic of free flight.

In 1988 Hans tested positive for HIV. At Christmas 1989 I came to visit him at his apartment on a canal called Oude Schans. Beyond his corner windows barges floated slowly by on their way to the Amstel River and the North Sea.

In Holland, Canada, and America, AIDS had tightened its noose around my circle of friends. I had already seen too much: Jay, who drowned in his blood when the KS lesions in his lung popped a major artery; Don, whose scrotum swelled to the size of a melon, and who would stare mindlessly at the ceiling of his hospital room; Tim, an artist who lay blind in pools of diarrhea, babbling nonsense; Larry and then Billy, hooked up to respirators and injected with paralyzing drugs, forced to wait as still as statues for two weeks until their hearts failed; Michael, who spent two years withering away to nothing; Artie, who after six months of unrelenting pain secretly and all alone took sleeping pills. Now Hans told me he had recurrent diarrhea. And he was losing weight.

We lay in bed at Oude Schans, sleeping late from a combination of my jet lag and our usual nocturnal forays through the ancient cobbled streets, and as the gray light of Dutch December seeped through the curtains to the interzone between sleep and wakefulness, I tightened my arms around his slender body, grimly aware in the passing moment that soon the flesh and bones in my embrace would also, like all the others, char and turn to ash.

On New Year's Eve — called Silvester by the Dutch — he took me to Nieuwmarket, a square dominated by two medieval towers. At midnight, as fireworks erupted across the city like gunfire, a dozen men pushed a wooden cart with giant wheels through the crowd. On it was a ten-foot-high wooden owl that sputtered and exploded in a catherine wheel. Then the flaming cart, piled high with fagots of wood, was consumed like a pyre.

"Four hundred years ago they would have thrown us on it next," I muttered to Hans. We had seen the execution warrants for seventeenth-century sodomites at the museum. Young men caught together in the act of anal sex, and methods of disposal.

Hans corrected me. "In The Hague, yes. And then they threw our ashes into the sea. But in Amsterdam we were only garroted in front of City Hall."

Hans's official diagnosis came a few weeks later. Cryptosporidiosis, which meant perpetual diarrhea, constant dehydration, and worse, an inability to absorb nutrients and medication. Thus began the double jeopardy of AIDS, when symptoms, medications, and side effects interact in a constant seesaw of suffering and futility. He went on AZT although it did nothing for him. Within months, a Hickman catheter was installed in his chest, and he began infusions of DHPG to stop the cytomegalovirus that threatened his eyesight. Then he began a series of long hospital stays with parenteral feeding to gain weight.

In November, with my help, he traveled to New York for an experimental treatment for his diarrhea, despite immigration laws that prevent HIV-infected persons from entering this country.

"I think it's working," he told me the day after he received the drug, Humatin. "It feels different down here." He patted his abdomen. By the third day he was beaming from ear to ear. He'd had his first real, solid shit in over a year.

With the diarrhea beat, he could absorb both food and medication properly. Instead of wasting, he began to gain weight. But neuropathy in his legs and feet made it difficult to walk. The world of the invalid is one of ever-diminishing circles, and his traveling days were gone. After his diagnosis the Dutch government had assigned him a ground-floor apartment with a garden, and he longed to return to it.

By the end of February the diarrhea had returned with virulence. Other viruses, against which Humatin was useless, attacked his insides. The DHPG that safeguarded his eyesight was causing painful side effects. He was losing weight again. The future meant lying in a hospital bed, in diapers, blind, and being fed through a hole in his side. It could have gone on like that for months. One night in April, crumpling under a burden of despair, he wrote a letter to his doctor stating that he wanted to die. The protocol had begun.

"I've had these three weeks," he told me, pausing and staring off at some invisible point in front of him. "Beautiful three weeks."

One by one, he began to tell his friends and say goodbye. Every encounter was different, he said, some easier than others. One friend kept making new appointments to come back to see him until Hans confronted him with his reluctance to say goodbye. The cleaning woman, leaving, said, "See you next week," but gently Hans reminded her otherwise. In the end, the irony was that the patient took care of everyone around him.

With one week to go, the doctor came to his apartment to officially examine him, as the protocol dictated. Hans questioned him persistently. What should he wear? Would there be a mess? Well, everything relaxes, so a diaper is a good idea. But no vomit. That was good. He could die in the same clothes that he wanted to wear in his casket. For those who inhabit the landscape of death, these matters are commonplace.

Hans became obsessed by the details of his death, which he studied with both fascination and a fear that his carefully laid plans would somehow be thwarted. "There are a lot of steps you have to take, and I think it's very good. It's impossible to do impulsively. On the other hand, it's important to think about it in time, because it takes a long time before you are in this space where it feels good. A lot of people, I know them from the hospital, want to do it this way but sometimes it's impossible because you can't make the decisions anymore for physical reasons."

In part, Hans's timing was determined by the medications he stopped taking when he made the decision to die. Control over his illness was "more important than being afraid of pain, or a shorter life," he said, and ridding his body of potent pharmaceutical concoctions gave him a burst of energy. But it was also like sending a car downhill without brakes, a strategy that made sense only if you planned on bailing out before the crash. Hans's weight dropped to less than fifty kilos. In a matter of days CMV would attack his eyesight.

Suddenly, the weekend before the Tuesday he had chosen, the wheels of the protocol ground to a halt. A second doctor was needed to examine Hans, and the one who usually worked with his primary physician was away. The substitute doctor refused to have anything to do with assisted euthanasia. No doctor in the Netherlands is forced to participate, but they are obligated to refer a patient who requests it to a physician who will. For a day, the sudden interruption in his plans worried him more than his illness.

Having launched a process and watched it gain momentum, Hans relied on that momentum to carry him through to its final conclusion. He was also in a great deal more discomfort than he ever let on. Most important were the closures he had already made with friends, places, day by day shutting down the world around him. The pages of his daily agenda for the year 1991 were filled with notes of what he had yet to do up to a certain day — and then abruptly blank for the rest of the year.

When he took his clothes off at night, his six-foot frame revealed ribs that were as slender as wishbones. His skin was cracked and scaly from prednisone, a steroid that stimulated his appetite and gave him energy. Still I wanted to feel him, hold him; I wanted to be sexual. But touch caused him pain, and as always the kisses I so freely gave I was loath to ask for. "I don't like my body anymore," he said. "That's why I want to leave it."

Finally a second doctor was found, and came to the apartment for the examination. The papers were signed. The protocol inched toward completion.

"It's very strange to live in this period, knowing that you only have so much time left," Hans said. "On the other hand it's so beautiful, so nice to . . . well, get there, to reach the quietness, the rest, the peace. There are no words for it."

On our last day together, the day before he died, he drove me to Utrecht to meet his father and stepmother — conservative, working-class people who lived on a houseboat moored in a canal. Between cups of sweet tea, nods, and smiles, we avoided the subject of death and the reason I was there. Our visit was brief. As we drove away, they stood on the road beside the canal, resolute, frozen and diminishing in the rear-view mirror.

We drove into the countryside, lush from rains and garlanded with spring flowers, taking a narrow road along the River Vecht, where Dutch merchants had built miniature Baroque palaces with round, cupolaed teahouses in the corners of the gardens. He said nothing to me, but a few days later I discovered it was the route he had chosen for his funeral procession.

We stopped at an inn for dinner, Hans withdrawing a large amount of money from a cash machine, laughing, "I'm plundering."

Despite all his preparations for the final exit, life crowded in relent-
lessly. Over dinner, he complained bitterly that although he had
promised himself that the last day would be entirely his — until
Marco and I arrived at six, and then the doctor — already he had
two appointments with late-coming friends who had prevailed upon
him to see them one last time. "To say goodbye," he said. "Is that
the right English word for this situation?" he asked. "Goodbye?"

"I like to say, 'Fare forward,'" I told him, and quoted from a
poem by T. S. Eliot:

> Fare forward.
> O voyagers, O seamen,
> You who come to port, and you whose bodies
> Will suffer the trial and judgement of the sea
> Or whatever event, this is your real destination.

"I feel like a whale swimming toward a beach," said Hans.

He rolled a cigarette, put it to his lips, and leaned toward the
candle in the center of the table. Just before the tip hit the flame,
he looked up, directly into my eyes. "I know, I know," he shrugged.
"Well . . . ," and with a droll smile he lit his cigarette from the
candle.

Marco and I arrived at Hans's at 6 P.M. It was still daylight, but his
rooms were lit by candles and filled with tulips. The table was
spread with breads and cheeses. Four champagne glasses stood
ready. He was still working at his computer, frantically typing out a
few last letters and instructions. He called in Dutch to Marco,
"How do you spell *attractive*? One *t* or two?"

"Two."

A pause. "I don't believe you," Hans stated flatly.

"So look it up in the dictionary," Marco called back, glancing at
the clock with exasperation. "I bet you one hundred guilders," he
growled.

A moment later, Hans continued his furious typing. Finally we heard the printer. Hans emerged and threw a hundred guilders at Marco, smiling, "You were right."

Marco laughed. "I think I get it all in a little while anyway."

Hans sat while Marco laid out plates and began to serve food. He seemed tense and withdrawn, all his resources, every ounce of his diminished strength pulled in and held against the impending night. Outside, beyond the glass doors to the garden, dusk gathered. As we began to eat, his eyes seemed cloudy with thought, and he looked at neither of us. We made small talk, incongruous to a situation that none of us had rehearsed, an event dictated by a fluke of viral evolution. He eyed my glass of beer.

"There's champagne to come," Hans said sternly. "Keep room for that." He rose, shuffled off to the kitchen, and returned with a bottle of Veuve Clicquot. He began to pry out the cork. "Watch where it goes," he said. He had a collection of champagne corks he'd saved from numerous occasions.

It popped with a great explosion, champagne spurting everywhere, and foaming into the glasses. Hans spotted the champagne dripping down my face and laughed. We raised our glasses and I offered a toast: "To all our journeys."

Hans nodded and repeated the words, quietly adding, "Yes."

We hardly felt like eating, tucking away only enough to appear polite. Hans popped a cassette into the stereo. It was the music he had chosen for his memorial service, and began with a selection from the opera *Peter Grimes*, by Benjamin Britten, the movement in which the sailor goes to sea. We listened in silence. For the first time in the week we'd been together, Hans wept a little, and with typical constraint pulled his knee up to hide his face.

The music had barely finished when the doorbell rang. We were expecting only one more guest. A moment later, the doctor entered. Unlike his visit a week earlier, this time he carried the small black bag that contained the means of Hans's destruction.

The doctor shook hands all the way around, and sat. Hans reached for his pouch of tobacco and began to roll a cigarette. He asked how much secobarbital there was to drink, explaining that the glass he wished to use was small.

The doctor reached for his black bag and undid the clasp. On top, amid the stethoscope and other instruments of his trade, was a small white box. He took it out, opened it, and withdrew a brown glass bottle, one-third full of a clear, syrupy liquid.

"Oh yes, no problem," said Hans, eyeing the quantity and nodding with satisfaction.

I got up and went to the bathroom as the conversation continued in Dutch. When I came out and stepped into the living room, Hans rose to greet me.

"It's time now to say goodbye," he said, coming close, reaching out.

"I love you, Hans," I barely murmured. We kissed three times in typical Dutch fashion, first one cheek, then the other, and then our lips. We pulled away just slightly, still hanging on.

I said, "And I'll miss you terribly."

"Yes, well, I think we will see each other again," he said.

We kissed again, our mouths open and entwined for the last time.

He took the bottle from the table and passed through the curtain that hung in the doorway to his bedroom. I took my place on the couch beside Marco. We were silent, perfectly still. Feeling my defenses crumble, I turned and clutched at Marco, burying my face against his sweater. Just then the curtains parted again, and Hans emerged. Quickly Marco and I broke apart, restoring our composure like children caught at mischief.

"I forgot my champagne," Hans said, reaching for his half-filled glass on the table. He looked at me with a bemused smile that was infectious, and disappeared behind the curtain again. There was silence, and then a quiet rustle as he got into bed.

"Are you still there?" he called out from the bedroom.

Startled, the three of us looked at one another.

"Yes, we're here," I called back.

"Are you smiling?"

Already his tongue was thick with sleep.

"Yes, I'm smiling, Hans," I called. I was. And then I called, "Fare forward, Hans."

There was a pause.

"What did you say?" The words came out with difficulty. The secobarbital cocktail was taking effect, like velvet hands caressing his consciousness, pulling him down to the deepest sleep.

"Fare forward," I called again. This time there was no answer.

Outside, darkness fell in the garden.

We waited in heavy silence, preserving the privacy that Hans had wanted to the very end; to go beyond the curtain while he lay dying would have been an act of intrusion.

The doctor busied himself by sorting copies of the paperwork on the table: Hans's letter, the physician's own statement. Soon, he would give these papers to the night coroner, who would come directly to the apartment, examine the body, and release it to us. The undertakers would come and zip it up in a black plastic bag. The papers would be sent to The Hague and examined by judges. Then the protocol, the ritual of the state, would be complete.

Hans died, officially, at 11:05 P.M. The doctor went into the bedroom first, with his black bag, and a minute later emerged silently.

"Is he gone now?" I asked.

"Yes," the doctor said, his voice sad. He sat and wrote down the time.

I got up and went through the curtain. Hans lay in his bed, curled up under the duvet as if he were sound asleep. I knelt beside him and pulled the cover down to see his face. He was dead. His eyelids drooped, not quite closed, and his mouth, still beautiful, was slack. An immense sorrow began to rise from my chest. For seven days, I'd concentrated on the time we had together. I knew death well enough to know that for me, the hardest part had just begun.

I dug my hand beneath the blanket to hold his hand again, leaned forward to kiss him for the last time, and felt his body heat already dissipating from his pliant lips. Then I fell against his body, and began to cry.

In the age of AIDS, I have learned that grief is a process of healing for what cannot be understood, the fact that someone has been ripped from the fabric of life. And every single death alters me forever.

With Hans's death, I became aware of perhaps the most important legacy of legalized euthanasia: that the ritual of the state, paperwork and protocol, and the personal ritual of an individual who prepares his final moment, allow that person to make a crucial distinction that has been omitted in public debate.

"That's just suicide," Hans said, referring to the men who, alone and in pain, have met their deaths by throwing themselves from buildings, slashing their wrists, swallowing mounds of pills, or eating the cold steel barrels of guns. And by that Hans meant that euthanasia is not. It is an extension of the patient's medical treatment, administered, as in Hans's case, by his personal physician.

In the days that followed, my mind's eye remained frozen at the instant Hans walked into his bedroom, the curtains at the door swaying like the wings of an angel. He took my breath away. Beyond sorrow and my loss, I saw a victory against a virus that knows no love. In the final stages of his illness, Hans wrested control back from the disease, refusing to give it any more of the suffering and trials that it demanded. Of all the deaths I have seen — and I have seen too many — only his had dignity.

[5]

Sex at Risk

THE BODY AND ITS DANGERS

ALL IT "THE SHAFT." Go beyond the metal door, up tall narrow steps, past the man at the top, and into a room that looks like an amusement arcade for sex. Forty men, naked, in jeans, leather, chains, have congregated here for all the usual stuff.

You see a handcuffed man on his knees, hunched over, head down. He loves to serve. And over there a man wrapped in plastic from head to foot, motionless, patient. Soon his master will start the unbandaging. In the bathroom a man sits in a long, old-fashioned porcelain urinal, watching other men pee. He wants to have some of that liquid spurting, warm and wet, across his flawless chest. Elsewhere, a man in a sling awaits the lubricated latex glove stretched up the arm of his favorite fister.

The Shaft's theme tonight is supposed to be "A Night at the Tubs," and a couple of men do actually wear towels for props. But usually the themes at the Shaft are just excuses for sexual gathering, the way a college fraternity might decide to dub this Saturday's blowout "Equinox Night." Sunday Sleaze, Tuesday Sucks, Thirsty Thursdays — they're nearly all the same. Tonight for some reason the men that showed up are more interested in having "Dungeon

Night." They line the walls of this industrial loft space, paired, tripled, quadrupled, bodies glistening with lube and sweat, fondling each other's dicks. The usual stuff. And perfectly safe.

You might find yourself shocked in the farthest room. Under soft red spots, a guy sprawls faceup on a banquette. His body stiffens and arches back, a moan of pleasure falling from his lips. A second man squats between his open legs, chowing down on his naked cock. It reminds you of the old days, in the years before AIDS. You don't know how you feel about what they are doing; you might wonder if the men made proper introductions and exchanged information about each other's serostatus first, or whether they have both soberly decided that HIV does not or should not interfere in their sex. Witnessing their communion as they perform what is perhaps the most central and sacramental act possible between men, you might even envy them.

In a corner of the upstairs loft, you watch two men play around for a while. One tries to back up on the other guy's dick.

"Wait, I have to go downstairs, I don't have a condom," says the top man.

"Just stick it in for a minute," the bottom begs.

The top smiles weakly. You can see him think. He turns the man around and, making contact eye to eye, pulls him close. Their mouths clamp together and pelvises grind. No penetration, just frottage. A moment on the razor's edge is disengaged. Not everyone is so considered. You can't be sure what's going on in the dim light, but it seems the two guys fucking in the far corner aren't using a rubber. Nor is everyone so lucky. Another man ends up sitting in a corner looking very unhappy. A guy he'd been sucking had shot a load into his mouth. It felt to him like someone had just pointed a gun at his head and shot it, with or without a blank.

"The Shaft" is one of several private clubs that have sprouted, been cut down, and sprouted again in New York and in larger cities around the country since 1985, when New York and other municipal governments first began closing gay bathhouses, bar back rooms, and sex clubs. No city has succeeded in shutting down communal sex. It is impossible to domesticate desire. Sex between men, sex among men, merely went underground — at playpens that draw their members from secret mailing lists; at tea rooms whose locations are passed along from urinal to urinal; at bathhouses on side streets, featuring gym equipment and "resting cabins"; at porn theaters where the action onscreen may be straight; at jack-off clubs that operate largely out of private lofts. But underground is a place where homosexual men have traditionally led their lives, both before and after Stonewall. Surviving sexual stigma and general horniness in the age of AIDS has proven no exception.

Even during the most repressive years of the AIDS crisis, a vibrant sexual playground survived in secret. The streets grew cold and scant, the neighborhood bars thinned out, but if you knew the right someone, you got taken to a place behind locked doors. Most gay men knew the right someone. The generation of gay men who have come of age in the era of AIDS are as fervent in desire as their disappearing Stonewall predecessors. In New York the night before the June 1994 Gay Pride Parade celebrating twenty-five years of gay liberation, the lineup of clean-cut, all-American men for a popular sex club stretched five blocks down the West Side Highway.

The truth is that gay men like to have communal sex — or, as it's called in the vulgate, orgies. Communal sex is to gay men what golf is to, well, other kinds of men: they find beauty and bonding in it. It defines the individual as part of a collective. By definition — because that is how history and social forces have conspired — "gay" is the construction of identity through sexual relations. The origin of the modern gay community arose in the simple act of two men picking each other up.

Experimental filmmaker Jerry Tartaglia, whose films have dealt with issues of sex among gay men, describes sexuality after Stonewall as an "alternative to a concept of masculinity based upon

hatred and competition. What was beginning to emerge in that collective sexuality in the seventies was a community built on love."
Men differ in their desires, of course, and desire different things at
different times; not all men like sex in groups, and for many men
anonymous sex is a realm they will enter and depart repeatedly over
the course of a lifetime. Many were in fact competitive. And for
some men, sex requited can lead to sexual compulsiveness and
desire unrequited, just as an intense focus on maintaining couple-
hood can lead to what pop psych calls codependence or love addiction. But for men just coming into the life as well as for graying gay
veterans, the values inherent in communal sex can be transcendent. Our sexual communalism has survived AIDS. It will help *us*
survive AIDS. For what we learn from the decisions we make
around communal sex can teach us how to thrive as a distinct, responsible, adventuresome, and caring brotherhood.

In acquiescing in the closure of bathhouses and sex clubs, the gay
community implicated itself in the temporary silencing of a vibrant
sexual culture. The alternatives we were offered — from inconsis-
tent or puritanical safer-sex guidelines to an insistence on romantic
love and monogamous coupling — can become dangerous misin-
formation in the nonrational logic of sexual decision-making. These
solutions have ultimately proved lethal to some gay men and their
lovers — and to the values of the community as well.

"What we do . . . is exceedingly controversial," says the news-
letter at "the Shaft," where house rules require latex be used for all
anal sex. However controversial, it may be less dangerous to its par-
ticipants than what goes on behind the closed doors of many gay
male bedrooms. While a multiplicity of partners in public can aug-
ment risk, what people do night after night in the supposed safety of
their own bedrooms allows for a greater sense of what is sexually
permissible — which can be lethal. A consistent predictor of high-
risk behavior for AIDS has emerged from numerous studies and

interviews in North America and Western Europe: the men most likely to engage in unprotected anal sex do so with their lovers.

Using a condom has never been about trust, but about the inability to trust. Condoms deaden sensation, taste bad, cost money, take precious time to put on, soften erections, and break. Whatever erotic value the condom had for us during our adolescence has been vanquished by terror. No matter how many rubbers we jokily exhibit unwrapped around bananas in safer-sex classes, no matter how they taste, and no matter how many throaty grunts accompany the slow roll of rubber down an erect dick, condoms remind us of death. They remind us how the intimate connections we seek can kill us. For straight people, rubbers are one of several possible means of birth control. For gay men in the AIDS era, using a condom is a means of death control. Condoms are a kind of closet, a barrier between us and the sexual aliveness we were prevented for so long from achieving.

They are also here to stay. What gay men nostalgically call "the old days" of sexual freedom are gone forever, constrained by the evolutionary tenacity of various microscopic life forms, their prevalence lubricated by our easy transcontinental travel. After years of fumbling with rubbers and lost erections, surviving grief and broken condoms, gay men still understandably resist acknowledging that "safer" is probably going to be forever — and many of them stray from the holy prophylactic path. And out of that terrible, sinking realization comes the plaintive cry of a young gay man, overheard at a Gay Men's Health Crisis workshop on eroticizing safer sex: "I just want a day off!"

Safer sex, after all its false starts, had worked; however much they might grumble about it, gay men had successfully achieved one of the most massive behavioral changes ever attempted. Yet that perception changed as early as the beginning of the 1990s. In November 1989, newspapers reported a 400 percent increase in rectal gonorrhea in Seattle. The AP story led with speculation that gay men were "abandoning the safer sex practices that protect them from the AIDS virus." The wire services were egged on by the Centers for Disease Control, which had editorialized on what behaviorists now call "risky sexual relapse" — a term for what happens when men who have made a commitment to practice safer sex "slip" from time to time by fucking without wearing a condom.

The term *risky sexual relapse* was first put forward by Dr. Maria Elkstrand, a researcher with the Department of Epidemiology and Biostatistics at the University of California at San Francisco School of Medicine. In 1988 Elkstrand analyzed data from interviews with 686 gay men in San Francisco. She discovered that a staggering 25 percent admitted to engaging in unprotected anal sex at least once during the preceding twelve months. Focusing on individuals, Elkstrand found that 9.7 percent of these gay men had never changed their sexual behavior. The other 15 percent had made a commitment to safer sex, but "slipped" a few times a year.

Whether it's sex, smoking, cholesterol intake, or not wearing seat belts — all of which can result in death — behavioral changes are very difficult to maintain over time. "If anything is surprising," said Dr. Elkstrand, "it's that there's not more slipping." At the international AIDS conference in Montreal in June 1989, while noting that the sexual adaptations gay men had made were "the most profound behavior changes ever observed in the literature on health behavior," Elkstrand introduced the concept to the world by delivering a paper on risky sexual relapse. Six months later, the CDC received the third-quarter statistics from Seattle and a little red light went on. The increase in rectal gonorrhea was numerically small — from twenty-seven cases to seventy-nine. But CDC scientists had their first data to back up Elkstrand's observations. A CDC spokesperson was quoted as saying, "These really profound changes — celibacy, monogamy — may be difficult . . . to maintain," a remarkably ignorant statement about what was going on out there, more wishful thinking than a take on the sexual activities of real people.

By the early 1990s the concern about safer-sex relapse began to pervade gay male culture. In his column in *Out* magazine, Michelangelo Signorile admitted that while on a trip to Hawaii he had engaged in unsafe sex with a military man. His thought processes revealed the calculation that many gay men use in making sexual decisions when they want unprotected sex bad enough to make a sexual calculation of risk. Signorile felt the guy was hot, knew his partner was military and thus was regularly tested for HIV, and had himself been drinking. His revelation in print allowed gay men to discuss more of what was happening to them sexually as the epidemic ground on.

Many of us were creating justifications more complicated than the ones Signorile made in his tryst with his soldier. Sometimes we made them at the Shaft, where given the number of sexual contacts in the room a slippage might have stronger epidemiological repercussions. But we also made them with that man we'd slept with twice and found ourselves falling for — situations where acknowledging we were HIV-positive, or -negative, could only divide us at a time when we wanted to come together. We might have unsafe sex again and again with such a man, getting infected and reinfected.

Except in HIV prevention workshops for gay men — and later in the pioneering work of psychologist Walt Odets in his book *In the Shadow of the Epidemic* — the human complexities around HIV and safer sex remain murmurs in the dark. In his book *Life Outside*, Signorile merely gestures at them while making a general analysis of gay male sociosexual behavior through snippets of interviews with bodybuilders, dance-party regulars, and drug users. There was little space for human complication. In the icy prose of *Sexual Ecology*, Gabriel Rotello concentrates on the serious ramifications of HIV epidemiology, declaring that until gay men have sex with fewer partners, the plague will continue, and that condom use is not consistent enough to contain it. He ignores the particulars of gay men's motives for sex. Rotello dismisses Odets's explorations into the reasons gay men choose to have the sex they do, and how they feel about it. In Rotello's view, gay men have unsafe sex and then make "excuses" for it. Ignoring gay men's psyches in favor of epidemiological inquiry while then proceeding to prescribe a curtailed sexual culture, Rotello commits a reverse version of the fallacy he ascribes to safer-sex education. In a book about the "destiny of gay men," gay men's voices are absent.

Among gay men, there lurks a silent chasm between practice and discourse. The real dope on what's considered safe has been suppressed by a pervasive shame — a fear of being seen as irresponsible, compulsive, or socially offensive if we talk out loud about what we are really doing in bed. Cocksucking? Is it okay if he doesn't cum in your mouth? Does saliva kill the virus? Then what about rimming? Is the gentle probing of a tongue high-risk? And urine, is it really sterile? Docking? What happens if someone's precum gets under your foreskin? Does HIV live in tears? What do you do when a guy whose beard is rough upon your cheeks begins to cry?

For many men who regularly engage in some of these activities with lovers or strangers, such questions persist. They cannot entirely be answered because nobody knows for sure. We gay men distrust our own institutional sources of information — whether they're the state health department or the local AIDS bureaucracy — because many of us suspect that their true agendas continue to be to suppress our sexuality and pour gasoline on our guilt. Instead, we rely on our own whisperings. The second tenet of coming out, acknowledging our homosexuality to other gay men, has long been ritualized in the continuing exchange of sexual information. Only there do we find reliable — or seemingly reliable — truth. We decide cocksucking might be safe because our gym buddy does it every night with his seropositive lover — and he's still negative. But what if our buddy is actually genetically resistant to HIV? Another of us, a seronegative man who is exclusively top, decides that fucking a stranger without a rubber is fine, and we kind of agree — until that friend confides that last month he seroconverted. We watch the seroconversions happen with friends — especially young ones, especially those who do lots of alcohol and drugs — and we know the issues around safer sex better than the experts. But we ponder these things among ourselves in low tones, with embarrassment and fear. As yet another generation of gay men come of age, ignorant of the ravages of AIDS and resentful of restrictions placed on their newfound freedom, and as a generation of AIDS survivors grow weary and angry, the tangled issues of what sex means, what safety requires, and what intimate choices we make or fall into remain for us to discuss in the dark.

At a Lesbian and Gay Studies conference held at Yale University, I heard activist and critic Douglas Crimp deliver a paper called "Mourning and Militancy." Awash in AIDS, all of us in that room, and gay men everywhere, were full of all kinds of grief, and not just sorrow at the dying. Crimp told us how when we mourned we were mourning not only for lost lives, but for what he called the lost "culture of sexual possibility: back rooms, tea rooms, bookstores, movie houses, and baths; the trucks, the pier, the Ramble, the dunes. Sex was everywhere for us, and everything we wanted to venture: golden showers and water sports, cocksucking and rimming, fucking and fist-fucking." His audience, from long-time sex radicals and professors to young men freshly enamored of Foucault, were primed for him, and they reacted as human beings, not scholars. Crimp's talk was received with applause so thunderous that he blushed and crept from the podium. For the first time I felt as if someone understood what I had endured as a gay man in plague time.

In his talk, Crimp told us that he had heard a young man, one who came out after AIDS arrived, say, "I'd give anything to know what cum tastes like — somebody else's, that is." "That broke my heart, for two different reasons," Crimp said. "For him, because he didn't know; for me, because I do."

One generation mourns. Another yearns. Both generations have decisions to make, based on nostalgia, longing, and hunger. All men take risks based on the intricacies of their own characters. A Stonewall veteran hearing from a young man, "Have you ever been to a baths?" or "What exactly was the Castro clone look? It involved mustaches, right?" could be amused were the questions not so poignant in the context of a generation gone, from a speaker so seemingly innocent of experience. It's only much later into the conversation, after the young man has told you what he's heard about, and what he's, you know, seen, that his eyes roll up as if to peer into the back of his cranium, and he silently finishes counting. "In the last six months I've slipped three or four times."

A young man in his early twenties points out with chilling clarity, "The word *slipping* is not giving it justice. If I know logically that what I'm doing might cost me my life, and I choose to do it anyway, that's not a slip. It's not like I went out and forgot to put a quarter in the meter. Why do I, knowing that this would kill me, have those 'slips'?"

The notion that AIDS is becoming a "manageable disease" — a phrase that first arose, appropriately enough, in the Bush era, and remains suspiciously reminiscent of the Reaganauts' fondness for "limited nuclear warfare" — may also assuage a man's fear when he's out on a limb and his foot feels air. He thinks of the antiviral cocktail that he believes will zap his HIV more effectively than an exterminator routs roaches. He is reassured by the word *cocktail*, so adult and glamorous, as if antiviral therapy were not a fierce regimen where one forgotten dose — one slip — can render your virus resistant; it seems instead like a Dewar's badge of adulthood, swallowed in some dimly lit medical lounge complete with sweet drinks and a jazz band. Yet another man, this one still HIV-negative, could decide that unsafe sex is all right because the object of his desire comes from a supposedly low-risk area like Canada, or Spain, or a military base in Hawaii. Another young man might figure he can stay within his age group. When one twenty-four-year-old Fire Islander announced about condomless sex, "I never let myself get fucked by anybody over thirty," he was instantly pounced on by a roomful of seropositive gay men over thirty who had all been infected by gay men under thirty ten years before.

At the other end of paranoia is a man who's afraid to share lubricant because of a cut on his finger. Or a man who's into tit play whose partner is rough and uses his teeth. His nipples are sore for a day or two afterward, which makes him anxious. "Who knows but you've got a microscopic cut somewhere? The way I feel about it, I could just drive myself crazy with all this." Or a man who will kiss no one, turning his cheek to his friends.

One man in his mid-twenties is baffled about why, after so many years of sex limited to jerking off with other guys, he wants to explore anal sex. Another man the same age struggles to find a balance between the belief bred into him that sex should only be intimate and never anonymous, and his equally strong desire for sexual adventure. Both men are genuinely frustrated — and too inexperienced and thwarted to have learned that an individual's sexuality has the potential to change, transform, unfold over a lifetime of experimentation and play.

Having safer sex requires not only chat about what you do but intimate negotiation about your health. Every seropositive gay man I know has been rejected at least once by a potential partner because he has HIV. I certainly have been. That prospect complicates what can be a fearsome exchange of information, whose effects continue to reverberate even if both partners are seronegative. Some men can elude this issue for months and call themselves lovers, their avoidance arising out of fear and discomfort or because they allow themselves a series of assumptions — he doesn't have It, he's so big;

or, he's too young for It; or, he's fresh in from Tennessee — that can lead to HIV infection. Along with all the standard relationship issues, the threat of AIDS adds an enormously complex burden, from lovers who unconsciously test each other's commitment by forgetting the rubbers to those who, enamored of the notion of casting their lots together, simply throw them away.

A young man told me of a two-year relationship that had ended a year before: "It's really easy to stop using rubbers after a while when you're having sex with the same person over and over again." A moment earlier he had claimed that he had never been unsafe. Inside the relationship, unprotected anal sex just didn't count as slipping, even though he didn't know his lover's antibody status. An HIV-positive man with an HIV-negative lover shakes his head in disbelief when he talks about how he slips. "Afterward, we always look at each other and ask, 'Why did we do that?' But then we do it again the next time."

One serodiscordant couple has never slipped, but they ache to. Calvin, the negative partner, feels limited by the roles he and his lover, Ed, play in bed. Because he doesn't feel safe being the passive partner in anal sex, even with rubbers, Calvin finds himself frustrated with the limits of intimacy. "Not only do I feel I can't be the bottom, but neither of us feels comfortable or safe if I go down on my partner unless he's wearing a rubber. And sometimes when I'm inside him with a rubber on and looking into his eyes, I want to be closer to him, just feel his warmth. But I can't. So in what I do and how I do it, I'm constantly reminded of HIV and the fact that Ed could die of this. Or me, if the goddamn rubber breaks, or I give in. For us, every fuck is a threesome."

HIV is not the enemy of sex; it's the antagonist of love. For two men to negotiate limits to intimacy admits an alien, third presence into the room, a virus that is almost tangible, always watching. When the need for flesh on flesh succumbs to unprotected cock-sucking, afterward both of you are spitting out saliva or reaching for hydrogen peroxide to gargle, wondering if this man with whom you've just been intimate could be your murderer. Or are you his?

One of my friends who came out as a twenty-two-year-old AIDS activist talks about what he has missed. His voice goes thin with frustration: "There are things like sharing semen that are very intimate. That's a big deal, to just, like, 'Oh God, let me just *be* with you,' instead of having in the back of my mind that the person I love can kill me."

The myth that romance can protect gay men from a virus may be the most ominous instance of a cultural collision between mainstream values and gay male sexuality. If we are married, just the way our parents were married, then we can't infect each other — or so we tell ourselves, enamored as we are of hetero notions of relationships. Gabriel Rotello discusses this in *Sexual Ecology* but focuses mostly on public-sex vectors of infectivity, which doesn't sit well with men in serodiscordant relationships, among others. "If I'm going to get infected," says Calvin, "it's going to be from having sex with Ed, not from hanging around in a back room. That may not be important to the epidemiologists, but it's fucking important to me."

Safer sex began out on the hustings: in sex clubs and S&M activist organizations. "I remember the first time I ever saw a safer-sex poster was in the bathroom of a back room, around 1984," says one friend. "I remember being startled by the idea that I should use a condom. It seemed so heterosexual — and sort of a turn-on." Safer-sex workshops are practically a cottage industry in today's AIDS establishment, but from the start of the epidemic, promiscuous gay men committed to safer sex became role models for slow learners and closet cases, and sex parties became forums for safer practices. In his essay "How to Have Promiscuity in an Epidemic," Crimp postulates that communal sexuality is what saved many gay men's lives when the health crisis began. Men were already used to sexual experimentation. Adding a condom to the routine, or exhibition-ism, phone sex, frottage — all were practices gay men could easily incorporate into an openhearted sexual repertoire. Crimp writes:

> We were able to invent safe sex because we have always known that sex is not, in an epidemic or not, limited to penetrative sex. Our promiscu-ity taught us many things, not only about the pleasures of sex, but about the great multiplicity of those pleasures. It is that psychic preparation, that experimentation, that conscious work on our own sexualities that has allowed many of us to change our sexual behaviors — something that brutal "behavioral therapies" tried unsuccessfully for over a cen-tury to force us to do — very quickly and very dramatically. . . . Gay male promiscuity should be seen instead as a positive model of how sexual pleasures might be pursued by and granted to everyone if those pleasures were not confined within the narrow limits of institutional-ized sexuality.

For public health officials, behavior change meant teaching people to abstain, be monogamous, or wear rubbers. Among gay men, more often than not it meant focusing on safer fetishes.

A club called the New York Jacks is perhaps one of few forums that survived the old sexual underground and have links to the new. The Jacks was a masturbation club, founded in 1979 by men who really didn't want to do anything else and, frankly, were tired of hav-ing their fetish laughed at. With the advent of safer sex in the mid-1980s, the weekly Monday-night gatherings became the right venue in a terrible era. The rules were simple: no fucking, no sucking, no exchange of bodily fluids. Held initially in the Mineshaft, and later in other bars along West 14th Street, Jacks evenings were for a long time closed to the public. A man had to be taken to three gather-ings by a member before he could join. As a result, these were emi-nently social events where friendships formed and men paired off in what would become long-term relationships. At its height in the late 1980s, the Jacks had hundreds of members.

Meetings were announced by mailings, and had an hourlong arrival time. Then the door was locked; no one else was allowed in. Usually a front area was more brightly lit, and men drank beer, greeted friends, eyed the room for new faces, and checked their clothes. Farther inside, in a space designed with nooks and crannies, and deep shadows, and low amber lighting, men came together, nude, in jockstraps or underwear, creating an atmosphere palpably thick with sexual delight. There was a kind of balletic movement to it, a strange choreography of masturbating men gliding slowly around each other until they came together in a heroic tableau of glistening bodies, the group growing in number, shifting and altering with movement, then groans, orgasm, the pleasure of men getting off on the pleasure of other men. The tableau would dissolve and new ones form, shift, and disappear, and almost everyone came away satisfied, no matter his age or looks.

With the bathhouses and sex clubs closed down, in these underground jack-off clubs men learned how to have hot, casual, orgiastic sex again — and how to keep it safe. Also part of the action, but not identified, were sex monitors, gentling people into the dictum "on me but not in me." While gay writers like Larry Kramer and Gabriel Rotello would join health officials to conceptualize behavior change as "getting into a relationship," at the jack-off clubs it was a matter of refining one's inclinations for voyeurism and exhibitionism, specialized loops of desire that might not enthrall everyone but can be very hot nevertheless.

Private invitational home jack-off parties became a popular bicoastal sport by the late 1980s. A how-to brochure from San Francisco — where the baths had also been closed — advised hosts to place plastic sheets over everything, and *not* to serve finger food. Many of the first private New York parties were given by alumni of the New York Jacks. Held secretly in club cellars, village vaults, Chelsea lofts, and Upper West Side apartments — ordinary places that for an evening became exotic, even sacred spaces — JO parties were extraordinarily social environments, and hardly anonymous. Some of the most popular were given by a lawyer and a doctor, lovers who lived together in a large Upper West Side apartment with panoramic views of the Hudson River. One night every few months they jammed the rooms with handsome, naked men. On one virulently hot summer evening, I was so coated with lube and sweat that I almost slipped out an open window.

A cottage industry of jack-off clubs developed, with brand names like SoJo, Hands On, and Jack Flash. These were run by small-time entrepreneurs who had mailing lists and access to loft space. On many occasions, the ten-dollar door fee went straight to ACT UP, the Community Research Initiative on AIDS, even political campaigns. Each of these private commercial clubs was known for a distinctive mix of guys. For all, the basic safer-sex creed was translated into Barbie talk: "No lips below the hips." A variety of men and body types was possible, but I recall a loft one night where white men wearing white jockey shorts milled aimlessly around and around. Standing next to me, the sole black man in the room said, "A little white bread here tonight." We both laughed.

What happened during the fearsome but empowering era of jerk-off clubs remains a model for how gay men can regroup to make decisions that can protect them, empower them, and keep them sexualized. Those men knew what they were doing when they manhandled each other: they had made a choice they could live with. Michael Callen — the self-confessed slut whose writings and activism helped invent safer sex in 1983 — wrote about "the exciting emergence of a new, in-your-face, radical, creative, friendly, hot, group-based sexuality, reminiscent of pre-AIDS sexuality." QW, the weekly gay magazine at the time the clubs reached their apex, editorialized that back rooms were "outposts of gay culture" to be defended "in the same way that we would, in an instant, defend our community centers." Gay men had come full circle, politically if not in spirit.

Now, in an era where gay men don't define safer sex so narrowly and where fatigue among older men and youthful AIDS ingénues allows for greater lapses in safer-sex practices, the clubs like the Jacks seem like innocence itself. As we struggle to reconstruct our identity as sexual creatures in the age of AIDS, we are edging toward a new sexual platform, one that is extremely nuanced, and rooted in values that are inseparable from that community of men called gay. Sexual decision-making has evolved beyond rigid categories of safer-sex guidelines to an ideology of shifting strategies. At GMHC's workshops, the goal has shifted from propagating rigid rules to giving men the information they need to make their own decisions about sexual behavior. Just as some sexual activities are riskier than others, so are some choices riskier than others. How much risk is a gay man willing to accept? How does he weigh risk against the measure of sexual fulfillment he wants in his life? Is he clear-headed, sober, honest with himself, and connected with the needs of his own body? What does sex mean for him, do for him? These days, every fuck, however one-on-one, is a veritable cocktail party of questionings and choosings.

Every exposure to HIV is a personal and communal tragedy, but in the shifting strategies of informed sexual decision-making, there exists a consensus about the vital need to address choice — especially when only the individual can measure the personal significance of certain sexual activities against their relative risk. SoJo Sam, who has operated a JO club, has put it this way: "Every person needs to sit down and say, 'All right, this is what I'm going to allow in my life. In the context of what I like to do, this is what I'm going to permit. This will be my code of safe, sexual behavior.' "

One thing gay men have worked out is cocksucking. Not too far into the crisis men realized that going down on a condomed dick is as pleasurable as wrapping your mouth around a roll of Saran

Wrap. No one likes to talk about it, but read their lips: most gay men are doing it without rubbers.

While no human activity is without risk, including driving a Volvo and staying in bed, only a handful of cases of HIV transmission through fellatio have been verified — vastly fewer than infections among health care workers from needle pricks. Most cases of seroconversion through oral sex have occurred among people who had open sores in their mouths and who had received ejaculate. In safer-sex workshops and among each other, gay men persist in questioning the safety of oral sex, which, as Walt Odets implies, has been a consecrated act of gay male sexuality and an intimate act men ache to reclaim. Many men have been persuaded of the basic safety of oral sex without ejaculation through the evidence provided by their own lives and activities. "I've gone down on a thousand men in ten years and I'm proud of it," says Tad, a friend of mine in his forties. "If cocksucking weren't safe I'd be dead by now, and I'm not infected. Same with my friends."

American health authorities are still far more conservative about oral sex than their counterparts in Canada or most European countries. In Germany, a safer-sex poster is a Mapplethorpian photo of a man's head securely nestled in another man's crotch, with the words "Nicht in den Mund spritzen": "Don't cum in his mouth." In England, an erotic poster of a blowjob had the word SUCK in large letters, and a smaller note warning people against unprotected anal sex. Other European countries and some health organizations and writers in American gay communities have focused on encouraging men to give up all anal sex and left oral sex pretty much alone. Rotello challenges this approach, saying that there is no evidence that getting gay men to feel more relaxed about oral sex will lead to a decline in the amount of more-risky anal sex. However, he does not make a successful case that oral sex — among couples, among promiscuous men like Tad — can lead to the kind of epidemiological showdown he otherwise prophesies. If every man had only oral sex with a thousand men and never eloped with a single lover, Rotello would have no choice but to be epidemiologically satisfied.

Certainly gay men value the kind of intimacy that oral sex provides. For all our talk of "on me, not in me" as the basis of safer sex, genuine intimacy involves, literally and figuratively, penetration. Oral sex is not only a sexual linking but a badge of that linking, a kind of nutrition. Also a kind of communion: in *The Culture of Desire*, Frank Browning quotes Bruce Boone, a onetime Christian Brothers novice who doesn't use the term glibly. For Boone, holding another man's penis in his mouth was a "dissolving of the self." "In Boone's quest," Browning writes, "to eat cock was in some profound measure to find the unity that divided the dictates of his spirit from the drives of his flesh." All of us, gay men both monogamous and multipartnered, have survived two decades in which sexual communion has not celebrated copulation but denied it. It has cost us more than we know.

Anyone who chooses to remain sexually active in the age of AIDS assumes risk. But for gay men, the stakes are higher and the terms more ambiguous. Is a man who has decided to forgo anal sex entirely but sucks cock regularly more at risk than a man who assumes the possibilities of condom leakage, spillage, and breakage in protected anal sex? If that man has protected anal sex frequently with multiple partners, is he more safe or less than supposedly monogamous lovers who have decided to go "bareback"?

Our community's effort should be to render all of those choices as safe as possible. It means that until there is a cure, some gay men will be infected with HIV. Contemporary gay liberation means embracing a destiny with which AIDS will ever be entwined. What people remain reluctant to accept is that safer sex means reducing risk as much as possible, but unavoidably accepting a small number of exposures to HIV, few enough to keep the epidemic from blooming.

This is what we had achieved in the late 1980s and early 1990s and must maintain now. This is no different from the way our society makes decisions in any other sphere: the tolerance of cancer deaths in exchange for a certain level of air pollution; the social approval given heterosexual sex even though it leads to a million and a half abortions per year; the number of highway deaths versus the cost to the auto industry of safety devices. It's a risk-pleasure, cost-benefit analysis, but that's how communities make decisions and legislators make laws. More people will die in this plague, and that's not going to stop people from affirming life by practicing their sexuality.

This isn't to deny that safer-sex campaigns must be ceaseless; that men don't "slip" or embrace "raw" sex without honestly thinking it out; and that the gay community has to grow even more vigilant about the transmission rate, our behaviors, and the communication of our values. Human females have always had to consider the personal health risks of sexual intercourse; regardless of orientation, in the era of AIDS and other dangers, human males are now forced to assume the same responsibilities. It's time to separate safer-sex education campaigns almost entirely from the AIDS crisis, because informed sexual decision-making is a necessary strategy for dealing with all sexually transmitted diseases, those of the past as well as next month's surprise mutation. Rimming is quite low-risk for HIV, but extremely high-risk for serum hepatitis and parasites. The development of new antibiotics is barely one step ahead of resistant strains of gonorrhea and syphilis. Herpes remains incurable, although there soon may be a vaccine. Crabs are a nuisance and the lotion can cause liver malfunction. Those who would call themselves sex radicals possess even greater responsibility for propounding safer-sex strategies so that, faced with unanswered questions, unacknowledged addictions, inadequate structures of the self, sexual self-hatred, and inadequate and homophobic sexual information, gay men do not make bad decisions out of frustration, in the blindness of infatuation, out of organized peer pressure, in a drug or alcohol stupor, or in the passion of the moment.

Engaging in unprotected anal sex is an extremely serious decision for two men to make, no matter their serostatus, no matter how much they believe they are in love. Taking advantage of someone else's sexual acquiescence, intoxication, or vulnerability to have unsafe sex, whether in a bedroom or a bathhouse, is morally wrong. Coming in someone's mouth without permission is reprehensible. As activists engaged with the sexual and psychic health of the body of gay men, we have to challenge those behaviors vigorously and lovingly in ourselves and others. At a time when microscopic life forms are mounting an evolutionary counterattack against modern medicine, all we have to protect ourselves are the limits we negotiate with our partners, the ethical standards we use to define those limits, and fraternal care.

The community has done better than the sex cops in keeping the virus at bay. Safer-sex practices originating in the community remain far more effective — not to mention affirming — than strategies of closure, repression, penalization of promiscuity, and enforced monogamy put forward by the state and by some of our bigtime thinkers. As Douglas Crimp writes: "All productive practices concerning AIDS will remain at the grassroots level. At stake is the cultural specificity and sensitivity of these practices."

Even in a new era when we are at once teased by hope and daunted by the war's duration, HIV transmission rates among gay men are nothing like what they were when the epidemic was wildfire among us. The efforts have to get even better if our behaviors are to help suppress the epidemic, even as we preserve the variety and values of gay male sexuality. We cannot let AIDS fatigue take its toll; the effort must never cease: to educate ourselves and each new generation of gay men to value our bodies, embrace all the safe possibilities of our sexuality, and make consistently sound decisions about our sexual expression.

When it comes to sex, for a century to come everyone will have to be his own activist.

It is inevitable that the reconstruction of gay men's sex lives will collide with powerful, erotophobic forces — from among our own, and from the media, from the straight people we so often scurry to please, from the government whose funding we must rely upon for AIDS research and care. As early as Seattle 1989, one behaviorist's "risky sexual relapse" has already become another social scientist's "recidivism" — a term conveniently borrowed from criminology. It wasn't long before gay men — in the process of reaching out to take the risk of redefining their sex lives — were beset by negative and reductive thinking on every side. Considering the relish with which the media speculates, the straight world was poised for signs of debauchery among a group of people still perceived as a noisy lobby at best, an abomination at worst. In the era of the AIDS cocktail, practically the only discourse around HIV that made the mainstream media was the controversy over the rise in anal sex without condoms, or "barebacking." By reducing homosexual difference to nothing more than sex, and then vilifying that behavior, our society keeps similar heterosexual activity in darkness and considers it an aberration; when it does bob above the surface of public desire, we cloak such heterosexual multipartner behavior with joco-serious euphemisms. While gay men made the most radical behavior changes in the history of public health, the response among heterosexuals, true to the silence surrounding their sexual practice, was pathetic.

"Miss Thing, there is no back room tonight!" replaced the usual listings in a June 1992 issue of *Homo Xtra* magazine. Squirt Farm, Comeback, Lick It!, Pubic Hair Club for Men — all were gone, thanks to a lurid exposé of gay sex clubs on the eleven o'clock news. Mary Civillo of *News 4 New York* tried to create a media sensation during May sweeps month by smuggling an assistant with a video camera secreted in a knapsack into the city's back rooms. *News 4* offered viewers footage of men gathered in circles, diddling each other; one shot of a flaccid penis; and, as Civillo put it, "what could have been anal sex" — a clothed man squirming in another man's lap. Although the camera caught nothing that looked even remotely risky, Civillo unraveled a lurid tale of sex and abandon in the secret cellars of the city. And the connection of most vital interest to the so-called general population was made when anchor Sue Simmons caustically intoned that AIDS was "an epidemic that's costing us millions to battle," perhaps implying that this expenditure gave society the right to control gay men's sexual behavior. "*Everyone's* concerned," Civillo gushed.

Many gay men reacted to the presence of hidden cameras in a back room as sacrilege. City health officials responded to the report with ostentatious casualness, and the attentions of the vapid and sensationalist local television stations flicked away to other equally useless coverage. Such media frenzies have stirred a public debate that has been entirely effective at diverting attention from the real issue: thousands of Americans struggling to stay healthy with HIV while science sleeps, snorts awake, and sleeps again.

Gay sex scares people. After the Civillo piece, a *Daily News* article reported that when inspectors from the Department of Consumer Affairs investigated the sex clubs just prior to closing them in 1985, they were so traumatized by what they saw — these sights remained unspecified — that they were forced to seek counseling. In truth, gay communal sex, even at its most debauched, is no more extreme (and undoubtedly "safer") than the behavior of heterosexual college kids at Daytona Beach or Palm Springs during spring break; the shenanigans of athletes, frat boys, and rock musicians; the escapades of American servicemen on leave or swingers in suburbs; or recent activities in a private study off the Oval Office. For better or worse, gay men reflect the sexual conditioning of all males in our society, no more and no less — from used-car salesmen to commanders-in-chief.

The NBC story was an indication of what would happen when Republican Rudolph Guiliani defeated Mayor David Dinkins in 1993. Guiliani's quality-of-life campaign may have made New York safer for the upper-middle class, but it has been widely criticized as oppressing poor people, sexual outlaws, people with HIV and other undesirables. One of the most visible and powerful guardians of public moralism in a nation increasingly rife with moralism of all sorts, Guiliani has been the target of frequent protests for driving sexual expression off the streets and out of the bars, many of which closed under his regime. New York's mayor may not have specifically targeted gay sex venues; he didn't have to. His critics say that he views public sexual expression — whether young black and Latino people congregating on the Hudson River piers or the innocuous delights of the drag festival Wigstock — as a public nuisance. His effort to pass and enforce laws that would drive every sex shop to the fringes of the city — to be conveniently located in such places as the periphery of Kennedy Airport — has withstood legal challenges. Certain gay sex outlets continue to thrive, including the fortresslike West Side Club bathhouse, curiously unmolested by the city.

In New York — and indeed in many other cities — communal gay sex has been driven indoors and underground, by institutional forces and gay male shame. The underground gay masturbatoriums of the 1980s were places where gay men learned safer sex, experienced it, and reinforced it through peer approval. Compared to the underground JO clubs of the late eighties, contemporary venues are dark and claustrophobic, devoid of sociability and accountability. Once the clubs summoned up the image of classical nude tableaus; today they are like conventions of flashers starved for contact. Rejections can be rude, come-ons too aggressive, the darkness filled with walleyed voyeurs or nervous gigglers; these are not places to admire social graces. They thrive late at night when more men are drugged or drunk, in an atmosphere of enforced murkiness where gay men have more trouble managing their own behavior and that of others.

Antagonism to the range of gay male sexual expression arose not just from the usual suspects — the glib media, a puritanical mayor, Jesse Helms waving a GMHC safer-sex brochure on the Senate floor — but from more well-meaning sources as well, who could pathologize sex, demonize gay men, and turn people infected with HIV into pariahs in the name of the common good. The primacy of "safer sex" guidelines over recommendations for abstinence in public debate represented significant progress toward a society that values pleasure. But those guidelines have been steadily appropriated by "professionals" who use them to purvey a fear of sex. A 1995 PBS radio show interviewed several psychologists who pathologized the compulsions that send gay men to sex clubs, listing everything from low self-esteem to Multiple Bereavement Syndrome. Omitted entirely was the most obvious reason: desire, not just for sex, but for simple human contact.

Professionals began to label multiple sex partners a risk factor for HIV infection, obscuring the premise that safer sex is about *what* people do, not where and with whom they do it. A paranoid and puritanical obsession with bodily contact has been inserted into the message. At a community center in one southwestern city, a lesbian group distributes "safer-sex kits" to teenagers at the gay youth group: a plastic bag filled with latex — condoms, gloves, and dental dams — and stern warnings against all human secretions. Confronted with a medicalized version of sex in a plastic bag, the eyes of gay teenagers register momentary horror, then glaze over.

Many gay leaders and writers did their part to jam the radio waves of gay men's desires. In 1997, Larry Kramer, who had been caricaturing gay male sexuality since his novel *Faggots* in 1977, attacked writer Edmund White in print for his novel of the 1970s gay sexual festival, *The Farewell Symphony*. Why must gay men always think with their dicks? Kramer asks, without telling us what's so wrong with the fact of our dicks or how we would be gay men without them. In the *Weekly Standard*, science writer Chandler Burr announced that if genetic alteration could make him straight, he would consider undergoing it. His self-hatred and heterosexism would be pathetic if they were not taken so seriously by mainstream media eager to declare an alternate viewpoint worthwhile merely because it is contrarian. Michelangelo Signorile, after chronicling the excesses of urban gay men preoccupied with augmenting their male secondary sex characteristics — men who, he does not much acknowledge, are often reacting in fear of AIDS and their own mortality — goes on to mention an alternative "life outside," a largely private gay life with its closet doors slightly ajar, where the sweet and vibrant urgency of gay male sexuality is at best confined to bedrooms. Just as the gays-in-the-military debate did in 1993, the movement for gay marriage has brushed aside concern for the continuing, unremarked disaster of HIV. One main argument for gay marriage — that it will "tame" gay men sexually just as it does straight men — is insulting, anathema to the historic truths of gay liberation, antisexual, and patently inaccurate. Marriage, just like most plans to curb safe gay male sexual expression, is one more simple-minded political solution for what is a complex psychological and cultural phenomenon: the intricacies and truths of queer intimacy.

Gabriel Rotello has called for thirty years of sexual conservatism among gay men, and suggested that the state has a role to play in enforcing that conservatism. In exchange, Rotello suggests, government should cooperate by granting homosexuals the right to marriage. He adds, almost as an afterthought, that society must also end discrimination against gay men. Such bright-eyed and bushy-tailed optimism constructs a dangerous Catch-22, because American society has a long way to go before it "grants" gay men such acceptance, no matter how paired or monogamous they become. Recent statewide referenda that crush the prospects for gay civil marriage laws are the latest mainstream suppression of homosexual legitimacy.

The campaign against sex clubs ignores a distinct cultural entity with its own profound normative values. Mark Blasius, who teaches politics at the City University of New York, has analyzed how gay men and lesbians construct themselves through their sexual identity and create what he calls "a way of life that connects our ethical sense." With that modus vivendi have come institutions and a culture of eroticism. "We come to understand ourselves through our sexual relations," Blasius has said. "One of the things that's always fascinated me about gay relationships is that you never quite know what it is. I mean, are these two guys lovers, are they friends, are they having sex or aren't they, what is their relationship to this third person? It's very, very fluid."

For many of us in the age of AIDS, second only to the lost lives has been the end of the culture of sexual possibility Douglas Crimp has memorialized. There was a time when every day on New York's subways, streets, piers, and in department stores, eyes met, glances passed, smiles were exchanged, and if both men were not too busy and one lived close by, there was always a moment for play. Street life meant an appropriation of public space denied to homosexuals in homes, colleges, and places of work, where heterosexuals can readily meet. In the "fairy" world, just beyond the gaze or ken of straight people, there was a constant individual affirmation of identity. Then, in the early 1980s, AIDS struck and eyes stopped meeting. A cruise too confidently returned could signal danger. The secret world of recognition that had bound individual gay men to each other had been stripped away.

Says SoJo Sam, "AIDS took it away in the form that it existed, but that hasn't been enough not to promote a new sexual platform that people really get excited about. I mean, I'm not talking about replacing fucking, but of a whole way of thinking about sex."

Picture this: men in white jockey shorts, in jockstraps, naked or with leather harnesses strapped across their chests like bandoliers. Their bodies glow under amber light. Along the walls stand solitary men, lone wolves preening, posing, or prowling. Languorous limbs, hands luxuriating through the forested chests of hairy bodies, frantic frottage — dick to armpit, groin to groin, sliding up and down the cracks of asses. Piss scenes. Dirty talk. Nude wrestling. Foreskins stretched in awe. A man twisting to fellate himself, a fireman going down on a priest. Spandex, bike shorts. Leather masks. Glory holes with disembodied cocks. Bad boys spanked by their daddies. Someone suspended in a cat's cradle of rope and hardware, his cock pulsating in time to the beat of his heart.

In these moments is a truth gay men have discovered: individual desire is as unique as a fingerprint. If they allow themselves to touch, safely, hand to hand, they can build an army of lovers.

6

Surviving Memory

TOWARD AN ETHOS OF DESIRE

A TANNED AND MUSCLED man stands on the beach in Fire Island Pines, looking out over the ocean. He wears black bathing trunks with a piratelike motif of white human skulls. Atop his head is a yellow baseball cap, crested with the grinning face of Mickey Mouse. Up and down the nitid beach this human metaphor promenades. His body is beautiful; even if he were taken out of context, no halfway-informed American would identify him as anything but gay, given those muscles, those ubiquitous tattoos, and that costume. In the glare, he seems as young as twenty, built beyond his years, this year's Prince of the Pines. But he might be older than forty, a veteran of this place and of the gay life it epitomizes, having come out here since, say, 1984, an entire lifetime ago. He saunters past a beachful of genetic wonders like himself, pumped-up flesh devoid of body hair, identical young men who seem to have been cloned in an Ecstasy freak's laboratory. Buffed and golden, they come and go across the hot sands, talking, if not of Michelangelo's latest magazine column, then at least of David, the fresh young hunk at American Fitness.

In my most heartless moments I see in my promenading man an

allegory for the generation of homosexuals who came into the gay community after AIDS arrived: loins bedizened with the leering, white bone face of death, heads loftily secured in the Magic Kingdom. The man with the crotch of death and the cartoon head is not just the sum of his emblems, of course; he is flesh and blood and irony and conversation. He is disease and risk. He and the men who look like him live Fire Island lives that contain an almost invisible distortion, like heat waves radiating, wavering and silent, up from the sand. One housemate's mild pneumocystis put him in the hospital for a couple of July days, and then his boyfriend totally freaked out. (That — and not, as gossip had it, a boyfriends' spat — was why one of them cashed in his house share and split halfway through the season.) Another long-time Pines denizen says he is fine and he is, his T cells flourishing and his viral load suppressed thanks to the protease inhibitor Viracept — which loosens his bowels only about once a day these days, in the abrupt and violent release he has dubbed his "Viracept moment." Another swallows thirty different pills each day, including Crixivan, which, he confides to two of his housemates, who tell the rest of the Pines, don't seem to be working anymore. His viral load has skyrocketed. He has, for now, run out of options. But he still looks enviable. And another man, the one with the heart and the sword tattooed on his left biceps, whose muscles arose from the steroids his doctor prescribed to prevent wasting, seems now to have lymphoma in the brain, which the fancy antiviral drugs can't erase.

One night at the Pavilion a dancer writhes through the sweat-glow of bodies to a nucleus of men, their inhibitions eroded by the love drug Ecstasy, gripped arm over shoulder and dancing in a circle. His shouts are barely audible above the disco blare: "We just sprinkled Courtney's ashes on the dance floor, if you want to come over and dance on them."

Beyond their muscles, their stories, and their prescriptions, who are these men? What do they remember of the ones who gave them this place and their pain, who bequeathed them liberation and HIV? Who were those original men? Of the generation that is dying or dead, and the generation that still lives — what will survive of them? With AIDS around them and inside of them, who will they become?

A few months before his death in November 1990, I sat on that same sun-broiled beach with pioneer gay activist and writer Vito Russo. He was supine on a lawn chaise, a kerchief pulled over his bald head, his skin translucent from the chemo that never did stop the KS lesions fulminating in his lungs. While we talked — about gay men, about our prospects with AIDS, about the first Christopher Street pride march he had led in 1970 — an airplane flew monotonously back and forth over the strand, dragging a banner that advertised with callous indifference the latest Bruce Willis flick: DIE HARDER.

That exhortation taunted the last of the Stonewall activists like Russo. It was not only their individual deaths they contemplated, but the extinction of an era that had been defined by the freedoms they had won and the choices they had made. In consuming nearly an entire generation of gay men, AIDS had rocked its precepts and challenged the existence of its collective memory. Vito knew this. He also had enough of a historical sensibility to know how repeatedly in the last century fledgling gay movements had failed to pass the torch before they were ground under. The work of Victorian sex pioneer Edward Carpenter, especially his essay "Homogenic Love," was suppressed after the trials of Oscar Wilde crushed the bud of a forthright gay aesthetic. The German gay movement of the Weimar Republic was extirpated by Nazis. In America, as historian George Chauncey has documented, nascent public gay life in urban areas like Harlem and Greenwich Village was aborted as Depression-era anxieties took hold. Twenty years later, the Mattachine Society was gelded by McCarthy-era witch-hunts. Each time,

gay leaders, writings, and stories were driven into a vacuum of silence, unretrieved until the years after Stonewall. In the face of a
mysterious and deadly plague, it was easy to believe that the same
thing could happen again.

Homosexuals may be born, but gay men are made. Among gay
men there is no continuity of memory as there is through successive generations of a biological family, where the mores, characteristics, and tales of the blood permeate the homestead like smoke
from the hearth. Nor is gay history transmitted in schools or in the
chatter of the media. Without the node of a vital, continuing gay
community, memory does not survive. In the earliest years of the
AIDS crisis, gay history and culture threatened to tumble once
again into a pool of collective amnesia. Once upon a time we tried
to figure out how we related to each other and to the men-desiring-
men who came before us. Now it seems as if we aim to elude the
legacy of Stonewall and ache to forget AIDS itself.

In the summer of 1978 I made my first visit to New York City as
an openly gay man. I met up with a friend from Canada, a North
Carolinian named Michael Lynch who taught American litera-
|ture at the University of Toronto. Immediately upon my arrival,
Michael led me down the island of Manhattan to Christopher
Street, pointing out its landmarks: the street sign at the corner of
Christopher and Gay; Bagel Land at Christopher Square, the then-
unmarked site of the Stonewall Inn and its eponymous riot in 1969;
the Oscar Wilde Memorial Bookshop, founded by Craig Rodwell
two years before Stonewall. On the other side of Seventh Avenue,
Christopher Street continued, a narrow canyon between tightly
packed brick tenements, the sidewalks bustling with gay men.
High over the tobacco store on the southwest corner, the enormous
billboard advertised Marlboro cigarettes, with a giant, red-lettered
slogan: "COME!" Beneath, in smaller print, it read, "To Man's
Country."

I felt as if I had arrived at the portal of a legendary city, the double-entendre on the billboard beckoning with promise that was almost mystical. That moment signaled the end of a long and arduous journey from the closet that had encaged me for almost twenty-five years, that led now to a happiness I had never thought possible. It seems naive to say this now, but the men I saw around me in those days were at once not just potential lovers but brothers, all of us connected in some basic way through the trauma of suppressed sexuality that had brought us to this place. Still blinking in the unaccustomed light, we had moved from a closet to a country.

On most days, Michael Lynch spent his time in various archives seeking traces of nineteenth-century gay life in New York, particularly as it pertained to Walt Whitman. He took me on long walking tours through lower Manhattan, pointing out the fruits of his research: a tavern where Whitman had once drunk beer; a parking lot that had been the site of a male brothel Whitman may have visited. One day, we walked across the Brooklyn Bridge and he recounted its history: how they had invented the technology for the world's first suspension bridge as it was built; how so many men had died during its construction; how the two neo-Gothic pylons — it's the only suspension bridge in the world built of stone — had been allegorized by a poet as two brothers, standing side by side and firm together, astride the cold, indifferent waters of the dirty East River.

Throughout the Western world, homosexual scholars like Michael Lynch were ferreting through the archives to compile evidence of homosexual men in history. The sources were often ancient criminal records and writs of execution for sodomites of centuries past. Until only a generation earlier, we had left behind few traces of our existence, save for the marks of our own oppression. Only a few years earlier the German Weimar gay movement and the writings of Edward Carpenter in nineteenth-century England had been rediscovered by young gay male historians. It was a complete surprise to many that the Stonewall movement was not the first attempt in the modern era at gay liberation. Much of this academic work filtered directly into growing gay communities, particularly through the medium of theater. The Holocaust play *Bent*, by Martin Sherman, which appeared on Broadway in 1979, and *The Dear Love of Comrades*, a play based on the life of Edward Carpenter and developed by the theater company Gay Sweatshop, presented by San Francisco's Theater Rhinoceros, suddenly made gay men realize that their desire existed in a historical context. Though it may seem something of a given now, especially for gay-pride cheerleaders, the idea that there existed some kind of historical continuity to male-male amativeness was one of the most radical notions of the 1970s.

The Stonewall pioneers were the children of Hitler's war and the Vietnam era, primed for protest and promise. Their lives were shaped by the conflicts and possibilities of the 1960s — a war that could abscond with your very life, a civil rights movement that sought basic human freedoms even as it stirred reactionary violence, and a fresh and unadulterated delight in the possibilities of the body. After the Summer of Love, sex invoked not fear but innocence and human connection for an entire generation of young Americans, including gay men. The sexual freedom of that brief bubble in time, extending from 1967 to 1982, with plentiful supplies of birth-control pills and antibiotics, will probably never occur again, and perhaps we are best deprived of our illusions. Yet it is important to remember that the credo of "Make love not war" was rooted in experience. We believed we were at the beginning of a new age in human relations — and we were. And the times, our reaction to our closets, and our trust in science all persuaded us that the risks of sex and love were merely to the emotions. We acted out of faith and out of received wisdom; we had sex based on our new principles, not out of abandon. Our license was licensed.

For me as a young man literally from the provinces, gay liberation arrived in part because young American gay men — too closeted even to seek 4F status from their draft boards — fled the United States for Canada during the Vietnam War. A gay discussion group had existed at Cornell University in upstate New York for several years before the Stonewall rebellion; Canadian students there and on other American campuses brought ideas of gay pride and collective struggle back after graduation. Canada offered certain cultural and historical traditions that were ideal for the egalitarian and collectivist community structures espoused by the new movement: the mainstream legitimacy of democratic socialism, which existed in Canada but not in America, where socialist ideas were entirely tainted by paranoid fear of Communism; the Social Gospel movement, powerful in Canada, that saw Christianity as a weapon for social justice; and institutional models of community ownership developed in the Canadian countryside by an established rural cooperative movement.

In 1977, I entered the gay community in Toronto by joining the volunteer staff of the *Body Politic*, a gay liberation newsmagazine. Although it had a circulation of only fifteen thousand, its readership was international, and since it enjoyed a reputation as an activists' magazine, its editorial policy influenced the gay movement in Europe and America. Founded with minimal money in 1971, the *Body Politic* grew into a sophisticated, well-oiled propaganda machine, its incisive and activist-oriented essays a harbinger of the AIDS activism of a decade later, complete with snazzily designed posters and exhibiting a preternatural skill at media manipulation. One by one, American alternative newspapers and small presses dropped their nonprofit, community-owned, nonhierarchical ideals in favor of private ownership. But north of the border, the *Body Politic* chugged along, its ideological purity caught in a cultural bell jar.

Michael Lynch was a writer and advisor for the *Body Politic*, as well as an essayist and poet, a founder of Gay Fathers and, later, the Gay Academic Union. The first time I saw him, he was a handsome stranger at the office Christmas party wearing an ankle-length denim skirt, the garb of a hippie earth mother. Outside of the pages of *Time* magazine, it was the first time I'd beheld "genderfuck," a form of drag popular with some masculine-identified gay men in the first decade of gay liberation. Although it continues to flourish in some rural enclaves even today, it has long since disappeared from the radar screens of the ironical urban gay media.

Lynch had moved to Canada with his wife during the Vietnam War to teach at the University of Toronto, where they had a son. Soon Michael would begin defining himself as a gay man. Activists saw as part of their task the development of new models of relationships among people of different sexualities and allegiances, so Michael and his wife tried to make a go of their marriage, but eventually they separated. Many *Body Politic* meetings that I attended were held in Michael's living room, in the shadow of an immense grand piano, as his eight-year-old son, Stefan, played amid the rumble of lesbians and gay men debating everything from bisexuality to the concept of gay socialism.

The velocity of change that the gay movement set in motion surprised no one more than these early gay activists, both Canadian and American. When they were growing up, they were deafened by silence on the subject of homosexuality. Every gay child was utterly alone, with only the barest of rumors to suggest a reason for his grotesque existence. His adolescent sexual awakening confirmed to him that he was the terrible creature his parents had warned him about, the boy-eating giant of fairy tales, the pervert whom schoolmates despised, a social outcast, God's pariah. And in the years when the activists of the Stonewall generation reached puberty, in most jurisdictions their desire was criminal. "If we . . . if we could just . . . not hate ourselves so much. That's it, you know. If we could just *learn* not to hate ourselves so very much." Those words from *The Boys in the Band*, a 1968 off-Broadway hit and later a movie, delivered gay men to the brink of the Stonewall rebellion. They pointed to self-hatred as the most destructive impulse in gay life. The response to those words — delivered by the friend of the host after he fished for a Valium to give him — pointed to the era's initially modest promise: "Inconceivable as it may be, you used to be worse than you are now. Maybe with a lot more work you can help yourself some more — if you try." For gay liberation to thrive, it needed to start by instilling in gay men a reflexive pride, which started with an analysis of the oppression we had been led to lay on ourselves.

The story of the burgeoning gay life after Stonewall is at once familiar and remote. Gay bookstores, social centers, theater companies, and health clinics sprang up almost overnight in cities large and small. Openly gay politicians ran for elected office and gay entrepreneurs built bathhouses and huge new discos. In city after city, gay bars began to sport plate glass windows facing the street; suddenly customers didn't care if someone saw them there, and the gay ghettos forming in urban centers provided some protection from vandals. The cavelike taverns and cocktail lounges tucked darkly behind brick walls became seedy and quaint vestiges of the ice age.

The gay communities in the 1970s also witnessed a clash of worlds old and new: older men accustomed to passing for straight, who detested the word *gay* and thought the movement only made trouble for "well-behaved" homosexuals; old queens who envied the opportunities younger men had created for themselves and threw themselves into radical organizations like mother hens; timid divorcés longing for "gay" with a suburban look; along with radicals of all stripes. Lesbians in the movement evolved in their own direction, finding at once solidarity, contentiousness, disdain, and denial among more mainstream heterosexual feminists as well as gay men themselves. The political crowd had cut their activist teeth in the antiwar movement or the Students for a Democratic Society; as the 1970s progressed, they often grew disheartened with coalition building, lobbying, and protest, as the first successes of the movement allowed comfortably out gay men to brush their broader political concerns aside. Now they began to cut their hair and shave their beards, reluctantly adapting to a look that coalesced around plaid shirts, Levi's, mustaches, and gym bodies, and was eventually dubbed "clone" — the late 1970s look that provided a sense of regularizing identity within the community and yet a distinctively gay look outside it. Hypermasculinity was an effort, at once ironic and earnest, to commandeer maleness by appearing more male than the norm — resembling the ideal of the heterosexual male more than he did himself.

As the efforts of the early activists fructified, more conservative gay men began to enter the communities of out homosexuals. They cared more about what straight people thought of them; to achieve respectability, prosperity, and civil rights, they ignored the radical and multicultural tenets of the gay liberation movement. They argued for assimilation in straight society, extending a vision of the out, "no-fuss-no-bother homosexual" who fit neatly into American life. Radical activists passionately argued against this rejection of difference. The Stonewall Inn riots had been ignited by drag queens, street folk, and all-around outcasts of all colors and orientations — people who had nothing to lose. The very members of the rising gay bureaucracy whose existence was inspired by Stonewall would now, a decade later, be appalled by the idea of a riot in Sheridan Square, just as they would have disdained the tactics of the Boston Tea Party two centuries before. As the visible gay community became more respectably middle-class, moving from the streets to the city-council chambers, the discos, and plate glass bars, many denominations of gay men were lost to public view. French theorist Guy Hocquenghem lamented the loss of "the traditional queen, likeable or wicked, the lover of young thugs, the specialist of street urinals, all these exotic types inherited from the Nineteenth Century." He saw them being replaced by what he called a comforting "white" homosexuality: "Gone are the sordid and the grandiose,

the amusing and the evil, sado-masochism itself is no longer anything more than a vestiary fashion for the proper queen." Yet as
early as 1963, when the modern gay sensibility was already well developed in major urban centers, writer Alfred Chester described
gay men in a New York bar as "mobs of dacron suits crowned by vacant, stupid, unlived faces, cute as buttons most of them, like an
army of Tom Sawyers. God preserve us from the invasion of good
fairies. Where are the screaming queens, the gigolos, the outrageous Harlem faggots?" Most recently, in his book *The Rise and
Fall of Gay Culture*, Daniel Harris has decried the decline of the
weird, peculiar, campy, and outrageous from prominence in a not-
very-queer community hell-bent on becoming marketable. Such
complaints are not specific to the 1970s or the 1990s, however; they
speak to the greater issue that the gay liberationists have left for us
to wrestle with — namely, who the hell will we be?

This split between assimilation and difference, what some have
called "the suits and the streets," has been a difficult dialectic experienced by anyone who engages with his or her homosexual identity. The dichotomy seems less a function of homosexual politics
than a manifestation of the character of modern homosexuals. Sift-
ing through the archaeology of the homosexual past, and comparing it to the new urban gay life, historian activists began to draw a
clearer picture of the evolution of the modern homosexual, even as
that evolution continued at a relentless pace. Where do homosexuals
come from? Why are they here? It was to answer such human obsessions that men like Michael Lynch scoured the past for avatars.

In 1933, a group called Harlem Hannah and Her Hot Boys
recorded a 78 rpm record. A husky, dark female voice belts out the
traditional song "Handyman" with all its sexual double-entendres:
"When my furnace gets too hot, he turns the damper down." On
the flip side they performed a less familiar song: "Keep Your Nose

out of Mama's Business (Mama Saves Enough for You)." The singer
tells her man that as long as she's keeping him sexually satisfied, it's
no affair of his if she goes with other men.

The Harlem Hannah and Her Hot Boys record is an example
of "race music" — early recordings aimed at the African-American
market, and the expression from which the slang term *racy*, meaning "risqué," is derived. The lyrics of race music were often heavily
laced with sexual overtones, some of them homoerotic. White critics paid little attention to black popular music, so, unhindered by
bourgeois respectability, African-American singers sang about what
they wanted to. The sexual double-entendre was a standard lyrical
trope.

But Harlem Hannah wasn't from Harlem, and she wasn't even
African-American. She was a white New York cabaret singer named
Peggy English. In the era preceding television, it was simple enough
for her to record as Harlem Hannah, and she was not the only
white female singer in the 1930s who went uptown to make herself
a name.

For minorities, the early part of this century was an era of pervasive self-oppression: "high-yellow" blacks tried to pass as white,
Catholics as Protestants, Jews as Christians, and homosexuals as
heterosexuals. By shunning their real identity, such people worked
to access the privilege and opportunity of the majority. Peggy English's transformation to Harlem Hannah, ordinarily a form of "down-
ward" mobility, seems to turn the idea of "passing" on its head. But
black women had one privilege denied to white women, and that
was the opportunity to project a sexual persona. By pretending she
was black, Peggy English was able to express desire in her art. In
Peggy English's secret transformation, we see the seed of identity
politics, not in academic theory or political ideology, but in how an
individual chooses to manipulate symbols in order to achieve her
full potential. Peggy English chose dissimulation, a kind of lie about

who she was. Her Harlem Hannah persona is redolent of commercial considerations, racial condescension, and the objectification and unfair sexualization of black people. But as a woman who, we can presume, wanted a measure of freedom to tell the truth about sex, all she could do was lie. It was the only way she could find a place to be true to herself.

Gay men and lesbians before and after Peggy English did the same thing she did. They adopted different personas so as to live at least a little truth about who they were. They could haunt Harlem or Greenwich Village, or explore highway rest areas looking like the truck-driver trade they may or may not have been; they could do drag. Or they could just have sex with each other and otherwise pass, adopting the protective plumage of their oppressors.

Early gay activists realized that gay liberation demanded *visibility* instead of subterfuge. Instead of infiltrating the ranks of privilege by assuming a disguise, liberation called for an abdication of privilege through the act of living openly. So fundamental was this act that a carefully delineated, developmental ritual of "coming out" was constructed to accommodate it; it's a rite that has become quite formalized since 1969, and one that forms the basis for much of the mainstream political ideology and activism. To counter the deeply inculcated self-hatred felt by a gay man or lesbian, early Stonewall-era activists developed a theory of self-oppression, which the London Liberation Front called the state of mind "achieved when the gay person has adopted and internalized straight people's definition of what is good and bad [about himself]." At its most insidious, self-oppression forced gay men and women to hate themselves with the intensity of their oppressors. This analysis was an important advance in how gay people thought about themselves because, as those British activists declared, it brought about "the realisation that inasmuch as we are agents of our own oppression, so we have power to overcome it."

To do that, it was necessary to seize control over how homosexual behavior was defined, and to define and communicate the identities of people who engaged in acts of same-sex desire.

For some gay men after Stonewall, their new visibility meant showing the world that homosexuals were the same as heterosexuals; for others, it meant showing how different they were. Harry Hay, one of the founders of the Mattachine Society in 1950, has claimed for years that "gay people do the same things in bed as straight people. It's when we're out of bed we're different."

Hay's idea is the cornerstone for those who embrace the idea of a unique gay sensibility transcending time, place, and culture, or the essential nature of being homosexual. In its most extreme tribal form, essentialism coalesced at "A Spiritual Conference for Radical Faeries," held at a remote desert ashram in Arizona in 1979. I participated in the retreat as a reporter for the *Advocate*. A blend of Wicca-influenced neo-paganism, Californian hippie sensibility, New Age, and ecological earth spirituality, with phallic worship thrown in for good measure, Radical Faerie "circles" sprang up across America and Canada, and thrive today. Their rituals are based on a kind of hairy sissyhood as means of empowerment. Much of the movement is rural-based in gay farm communes, a branch of the tribe served by the magazine *RFD*. Among Radical Faeries, the body and sex are sacred. In the words of an aretology attributed to the Great Goddess, "All acts of love and pleasure are my ritual."

For Hay and other Radical Faeries, gay men are possessed of a particular spiritual vocation. John Burnside, Harry Hay's companion of many years and another early figure in the Radical Faerie movement, argues that gay people are responsible for the "evolution of culture" in their societies — an analysis inspired by his knowledge of the berdache, the effeminate, cross-dressing, and homosexually behaving shamans in American Indian tribes. For many gay men, the berdache remains an attractive character. She / he had an inte-

◆ SURVIVING MEMORY

gral, specific, irreplaceable role to play in the life of the tribe —
unlike contemporary assimilated Western gay men, whose cultural
role has been to be the hero's best friend, the girl who doesn't get
the guy. The homosexual as poodle.

Harry Hay and his fellow Faeries were among the first organized
post-Stonewall homosexuals to view gay sensibility as a kind of
essence, one that arose consistently, if with different coloring, in
different times, places, and cultures. Today the supports for the essentialist position are found in fields that seem mutually exclusive:
the spiritual metaphysics of Radical Faeries, the work of genetic scientists to find the biological origins of homosexuality, and civil
rights organizations who hope straight people will hate gay people
less if they believe we never chose to be homosexual (and, it must
be presumed, that we would never have made a choice to be so
perverse, alien, and alienated). Quite apart from the image of gay
men dancing in the desert in denim skirts, the idea of a genetic
basis for sexual orientation is appealing because it offers a "no-fault
homosexuality." If your kid is queer, you no longer have to cru-
cify yourself over "what went wrong" when you reared your child.
Instead, you can take comfort in the mysterious and uncontrollable
confluences of DNA — until, of course, scientists decode those genetic mysteries and arrange to provide you with a bouncing baby
heterosexual.

Structuralist concepts of sexuality have challenged essentialism
on every front. Structuralists see all desire as particular to time and
place, distinct yet mutable fabrications based on a confluence of social conditions. What united a berdache tribesman and a bearded
gay farmer telling stories around a campfire would, for those theorists, be nothing more elemental than a sex act. Yet essentialism remains popular in the gay community, partly because structuralist
ideas about homosexuality contradict a basic tenet of the gay identity politics: that collectively, homosexuals have created a common
culture and community.

The concept of homosexuality as a characteristic, not a condition, is a new and fragile one, not even as old as the twentieth century. Our enemies are still enamored of the idea that homosexuality is not a way of being but a strategy of seduction. Homosexuals recruit, we are told, and young men and women can fall into the life as if it were alcoholism, socialism, or bad posture. Such ideas are not the intellectual property only of the religious right. International law now recognizes gay men and lesbians as a particular "social group," but in Cincinnati in 1994, when gay leaders brought a lawsuit to overturn a referendum revoking a municipal antidiscrimination clause, a judge held that homosexuals did not constitute a community and dismissed the case. This dangerous contradiction between "queer" theory and a gay rights strategy caused one structuralist, Diane Fosse of Princeton, to put forth what she has called "strategic essentialism," a position she has since repudiated. In short, strategic essentialism sees identity politics as a ploy to help the gay movement attain certain of its goals.

Though scientists continue to grope for answers, probing the hypothalamus and the dense necklace that is DNA, no evidence exists for a genetic basis for sexual orientation, any more than it does for any single psychosocial phenomenon. Nor would the so-called gay gene tell us anything about a connection between berdache sacred dancing and contemporary adulation of Barbra Streisand. A 1993 study in *Archives of General Psychiatry* notes, however, that "temperamental and personality traits interact with the familial and social milieu as . . . sexuality emerges. . . . Such traits may be heritable, or developmentally influenced by hormones." Some research does support the idea that developmentally, gay men differ in more than their sexual decision-making. A Canadian study indicated that the nature of gay men's cognitive skills falls between the extremes of those of male and female heterosexuals, perhaps indicating that the brains of homosexual men are organized differently. The investigator noted that this "may explain why there appears to be a preponderance of homosexuals within certain professions."

In the earliest gay liberation writings, the question, Where do homosexuals come from? was seen as a manifestation of self-oppression. Our origins, the first activists claimed, don't matter. What does matter is the reconstruction of our society's organization of desire in a way that allows homosexual men and women equality, freedom, the opportunity to realize their full potential as human beings, and the ability to contribute to the larger community. In other words, the important question is, How do we wish to define ourselves?

The Radical Faeries presented a vision of meaning for homosexual men as they relate to society. These beliefs in difference are, to some extent, the defense of the little guy against marginalization. They thrive on significant gestures. The bearded drag queen is not gender itself but genderfuck; he is not the populace but the protest. Were there other means through which gay men could express what just might be their essential selves, and do it on Main Street, Fifth Avenue, or on television?

It became increasingly clear in the decade after Stonewall that no matter how visible gay men made themselves in their daily lives, they were consistently rendered invisible except when reduced to genital behaviors. They were noted to have style but not sensibility, sex but not sexuality. Even as it nodded a reluctant hello to gay sex, society defended its traditional constructions of sexual desire and homophobia with a *system of refusal*, an unwillingness to recognize homosexual men and women as a particular, challenging, and rightfully queer element of American society and civilization. This system of refusal remains the mainstream Maginot Line against the kind of change that gay liberation demands. Such enforced invisibility is more than just transforming Divine into Miss Piggy, or Andy Warhol into an asexual pixie for mainstream consumption.

At its most severe, it reduces homosexual men to their sexual behavior alone, ensuring their pariah status. For Western culture is fundamentally erotophobic — that is, afraid of erotic love and human carnality, and attributing to it the most damning of responsibilities: the Fall from heavenly grace. As the French theorist Michel Foucault pointed out, our civilization is not sexually repressed, it is sexually obsessed. This obsession is driven by fear.

In his book *Culture Clash*, cultural critic Michael Bronski writes: "Erotophobia is such a tenacious strain of Western culture that it affects every aspect of our lives . . . our attitudes towards women, children, race, class and . . . sexuality in general. It has perpetuated strict sexual and gender roles which in turn support and reinforce the erotophobia which fostered them. Homosexuality, with its blatant disregard for sexual assignments, flies in the face of this system."

The defense of the predominant, erotophobic system of desire is accomplished through what early gay radical Arthur Evans called "containment and regulation." The system of refusal is the tissue that binds the attempt to neuter Ellen DeGeneres on television with public contempt for sadomasochistic practices; it connects the suppression of bathhouses and outdoor sex with the inability of the nation's schools even to acknowledge homosexuality and with the elevation of an overtly homophobic military caste. It is a system of refusal that vitiates declarations of visibility and desexualizes desire.

As gay historians followed erotophobia back into history, from the ancient suppression of paganism to the witch burnings of medieval Europe and the Renaissance executions of sodomites, they began to realize that homosexuals have been the losers in a two-millennium war against Eros. The official history of our culture has been written from the victor's antierotic point of view.

Then came AIDS. With the advent of "gay cancer," newly emancipated homosexual men were handed a different kind of "difference" from the one that some of them had been seeking. Gay men were a product of the same antisexual culture their persecutors were. AIDS tapped into their erotophobic conditioning and self-oppression and created among them a kind of generalized panic. Writing in the pages of the *Body Politic* in 1982, Michael Lynch warned of this panic: "It could never have set in so quickly and so deeply if within the hearts of gay men there weren't already a persistent, anti-sexual sense of guilt, ready to be tapped."

That same year, Michael Lynch threw a cocktail party at his Toronto home for Michel Foucault. The publication of the first volume of Foucault's *History of Sexuality* in 1980 had created a buzz among activist academics. In the years since its publication, Foucault has been deified by the academy. The debate that for the early gay liberationists had been framed between assimilation and difference was now recast by the introduction of French linguistic theory and its irksome hieratic language. The Radical Faeries had a whole new vocabulary available to them, if they ever wanted to adopt it. Henceforth, the "discourse" that preoccupied high-end academics was between the poles of the social construction of sexuality and the essential nature of identity. Social constructionism posits that identity is entirely a social creation, "constructed" by history, culture, and individuals. Essentialism suggests that there is something inherent about being gay that precedes individual identity. Because essentialism has been used to justify women's supposedly inherent calling to be child bearers, and dark-skinned people's being deemed slaves, the concept entered gay theory laden with suspect baggage.

Foucault was lecturing at the University of Toronto for the month of June 1982. Michael's party, more than anything, was to introduce him to the leaders of the city's gay institutions. Foucault was an odd and unattractive man, short, completely bald, dressed always in the black leather garb of an S&M daddy. He wore an expression as blank and undifferentiated as the label on a can of generic vichyssoise. He spoke no English, and almost as little French, rarely involving himself in a conversation. His student chaperons nervously reassured everyone that Foucault was "so brilliant everything bores him!" Foucault's eyes, when not entirely affectless, were sometimes wet and almost beseeching; for all the world he could look like a motherless child. His lover, Daniel, was his opposite, vivacious and gregarious; he acted as the eccentric writer's enabler. A story circulated that one prestigious American university had arranged for Foucault to lecture, but Foucault had forgotten to go. Forewarned, the University of Toronto had relied on Daniel to get him across the Atlantic Ocean on time.

Activist historians like Michael Lynch had pored through nineteenth-century texts, tracing the lives of women and men who desired the bodies of their own sex, chronicling the namings given to them and to their bonds and relationships: "inverts" and "urnings," "adhesiveness," and "the dear love of comrades." Foucault's work codified the predominant strain of historical thought: that "homosexuals" had been "invented" and were unique to Western industrial society. In Foucault's words, homosexuality concerned behavior, not the persons who engaged in it; when the nineteenth century began medically characterizing everything, the homosexual person became a "species."

Foucault pointed out that different societies organize sexual desire and the body's pleasures in different ways. European-American cultures possess a dichotomy of heterosexuality and homosexuality, stigmatizing same-sex partners. Many cultures — Latin American, Arabic, Japanese — organize desire into active and passive, stigmatizing receptive behavior regardless of the sex of the partners. Still other cultures have organized desire in generational terms — classical Greece, and certain modern-day cultures in Melanesia. In our society, of course, intergenerational sex is one of the greatest taboos, severely punished when it involves a person under age eighteen, and often ridiculed when there is more than a decade or two of age difference between adult partners.

Many gay activists deeply resented these incursions of French theory into home-grown North American politics. Entire areas of debate were abruptly closed off. According to structuralists, since homosexuality is neither cross-cultural nor transhistorical, it is impossible to compare homosexual behavior across such impermeable boundaries. While essentialists might claim Socrates and Alexander the Great as homosexuals, structuralists assert that this is nonsense: the behavior of ancient Greeks cannot be compared with that of late twentieth-century denizens of South Beach. While essentialists argue that a gay sensibility can be found, say, in the music of Schubert, structuralists dismiss this as impossible because the category "gay" has existed for only a few decades of the twentieth century. Theorists who followed in Foucault's footsteps have been, as he was, obsessed by labeling and being labeled, and with the individual's inevitably futile attempt to break free of classification.

One Friday night shortly after Michael's party, I ran into Michel Foucault and Daniel downtown, aimless and gawking on a busy street corner. They recognized me and accompanied me to an old-fashioned gay bar called the St. Charles Tavern. The place was a relic of old-time Canada, the only gay bar in Toronto that had survived the era before Stonewall into the eighties. The bar was still licensed to sell liquor under the strict laws that followed prohibition. One side, where hustlers now trolled, was a cocktail lounge restricted to "ladies and escorts," while the other side was a tavern for men, serving only draft beer. All patrons had to sit together at tables, because the archaic laws forbade standing or walking with a drink. Rotund waiters strode between rows of tables, their battered steel trays carrying dozens of foaming glasses. At fifty cents a glass, patrons ordered five or ten beers at a time, holding up a hand with fingers spread to signal how many they wanted.

The clientele spanned the generations, from elderly, closeted men to teenage hustlers and rough trade; a few middle-class white boys indulging their *nostalgie de boue*; sexually ambiguous black men from Caribbean countries; and drag queens of all descriptions. The air was smoky, the atmosphere chaotic. There were occasional knife fights in the bathrooms and bloodstains on the floor. A potted palm tree struggled for survival near an ancient jukebox with a vintage selection.

When we entered and took a seat, Foucault's face remained set with marmoreal indifference. Daniel prattled on, curious and loquacious, while Foucault impassively regarded the bizarre characters parading up and down the long aisle between the tables. Then I did something completely without thought, a gesture from my college days in small provincial cities when I drank in blue-collar taverns. There was a large saltshaker on the table. I dashed some across the surface of my beer, lifted my glass, and with a practiced stroke slammed the thick bottom sharply on the table. The cold draft beer immediately effervesced, forming a thick head of foam. Foucault's eyes bulged, and with the kind of disordered panic that the French reserve for the gastronomically incorrect, he began to sputter and ask questions, fascinated and perhaps repelled by the notion of salt in beer. In the deconstruction of identity — in my case, a national and working-class identity — the most picayune details can be exceptionally important. They can give you away.

This is the flaw in the dissembling that Peggy English revealed every time her accent skewed into Northeast Caucasian. It is a flaw assimilationists expose every time they look at their fingernails the wrong way. Assimilation forces you to assume an identity that has been determined by the power of history. When she sang as Harlem Hannah in a recording studio more than half a century ago, the self-oppressive specter standing behind Peggy English was a white, heterosexual male, representative of an erotophobic society that denied women's sexual pleasure and could appreciate it only under the guise of a black woman that society devalued even more than it did her Caucasian female comrade. Living under the regime of a false identity means a life lived in terror of the fatal "slip" that reveals the utmost secret. It's not the big things that betray people's true identity; it's little things as innocuous as salting beer.

In a world where power remains in the hands of a social and psychic Great Father, assuming a new mask offers only an illusion of safety. The mother of a Jewish friend, a woman whose family did not survive the Holocaust, put the same thing differently when she saw her son losing his religion: "No matter who you try to be, when the knock comes on the door at four in the morning, you're just a Jew."

When others have the power to define your difference for you, they hold sway over the quality of life and can determine who lives or dies. At the St. Charles Tavern with Michel Foucault, my difference was homespun and merely quaint. In terrible times, differences of identity can be a death sentence. "We never, until the war, thought of ourselves as Muslims," a Bosnian has said. "The definition of who we are today has been determined by our killers . . . this means these Serbs have won." Gide wrote: "It is better to be hated for who you are than loved for who you are not." Passing through life in an assumed identity — black woman or man as white, Jew as gentile, gay as straight — can be the mark of a survivor, but it is also the worst form of self-oppression. It murders who the individual really is by rendering the stigmatized identity invisible, and does the work of the oppressor for him.

If you can take on a name for yourself, you can have some mastery over your own identity. Gay activists realized this from the beginning, and enshrined it in the name of their new politic movement. Unlike *faggot, sodomite, fairy, sissy,* and even that favorite of theorists and early 1990s activists, *queer,* the word *gay* bubbled up from homosexual subculture; it was the name homosexual men used to talk about themselves. Gay men did not start the naming, but as long as others had labels for them, they insisted on having their own.

Here is an identity: *I am HIV, as much literally in the genetic codes of my cells as in the figurative way that HIV will define me for the rest of my life.*

To those people in power who would label homosexuality a pathology, which is to say most people in power, with the advent of AIDS the homosexual had a new definition: purveyor of plague. *My blood and semen are poison to my species.* Gay men could collude in propagating a model of AIDS in which the virus was 100 percent effective, infection necessitated death, and death was deserved. For those who were infected and those who were not, AIDS could be a solution to homosexuality as effective as execution by fire or garrote, as efficient at erasing a problematic identity as hormone treatment, born-again sexual reparation therapy, and psychoanalysis were not.

AIDS made the gay community particularly vulnerable to its own collective self-oppression. We had been out in the world for only a decade; the foundations had barely been poured for the edifices of community and self-identity we aimed to erect. Self-oppression underlay the position many gay men took in favor of closing the bathhouses in the epidemic's first dark days. Michael Lynch tried to analyze why gay men in New York had so readily fallen into "the medicalization trap," where they would reflexively define themselves by their disease. He suggested that they were "ripe to embrace a viral infection as a moral punishment." Such deeply inculcated self-oppression, Lynch declared, allowed gay men to give up their right of naming: "Like helpless mice we have peremptorily, almost inexplicably, relinquished the one power we so long fought for in constructing our modern gay community: the power to determine our own identity."

For a group of gay men lulled by the liberal and false belief in historical progress, by a measure of economic security, and by a belief in the inevitability of justice, AIDS was, as one activist put it, "the plot twist that no one expected." Because of his Fire Island friendships Michael Lynch knew some of the first men with AIDS. He saw, even before there was an officially named virus, that the so-called gay cancer would spread from New York, and that gay communities everywhere had to be prepared for that. And he knew that gay men would have to seize the power of naming, to create an identity around it. He wrote: "We have to make illness gay, and dying gay, and death gay, just as we have made sex and baseball and drinking and dressing gay. This is the challenge to us in 1982."

Hello, Mom and Dad? I've got good news and bad news. The bad news is that I'm gay; the good news is that I'm dying.

AIDS is the greatest "outer" of them all — from Rock Hudson to Roy Cohn to Rudolf Nureyev, all of whom concealed their sexuality and sickness, to Randy Shilts and Robert Massa, who hid their HIV status while writing about AIDS until physical signs of their illness became apparent.

Virtually all gay men who discover they're HIV-positive repeat the coming-out ritual they had rehearsed when they accepted their sexual orientation. This time, however, they confront the moral metaphors of disease and the socially edifying equation that pleasure has its price. The labeling wars began almost as soon as the epidemic did, with the early terms for the syndrome *gay cancer* and *Gay Related Immune Deficiency*, which were discarded less because they were homophobic than because they turned out to be epidemiologically inaccurate. Soon, the phrase *AIDS victims* was replaced in progressive parlance with *people with AIDS*, a battle of words that led to the founding of national and local PWA coalitions in Denver in 1983. Neither *PWA* nor its successor term, *people living with AIDS*, gets consistent play from the government or mainstream media; they remain designations in use mostly by people in the HIV community. Gay people not only had to confront AIDS victimology; they also had to confront the characterization of pediatric AIDS cases as "innocent," with the implication that all other AIDS cases were somehow guilty.

As gay men began to recover from the first body blows, they did begin to reject the narratives of inevitable death that the American establishment handed them. Soon AIDS treatment activism began, with buyers' clubs and contraband pharmaceuticals in defiance of the FDA. Long-term survivors put their facts and their faces before the public to rebut the presumptions of doom. If the idea that our bodies belonged to ourselves was a revolutionary notion in the 1960s and 1970s, then the gift to society from the AIDS generation was the myth-shattering concept that people with a life-threatening condition had a right to treatments of their choice.

The politics of the Stonewall-era gay movement shaped the gay community's response to AIDS, but the same social forces that deny the legitimacy of the gay movement were also dragged into the arena — in particular, the system of refusal. At the beginning, mainstream powers-that-be denied the existence of a health crisis, and even a need for urgency or government assistance. Through malign neglect — no, criminal intent — the same establishment that had long neutered and marginalized gay men now would let them die. In 1985, to counter the system of refusal and to garner broad-based support and more government funding, AIDS activists made a strategic decision to sell AIDS as "everyone's disease" — despite much epidemiological evidence that it would continue to affect primarily gay men, IV drug users, and their sex partners. Now, to circumvent America's silence, AIDS would not be pitched as a "gay disease" at all. Fighting AIDS would not be linked to demanding a place in America for gay men and their queer sensibility and unnerving sexuality. Probably, given the effectiveness of the system of refusal in the years before AIDS, such a battle would have been impossible to wage successfully. But what made the outcome even more painful was what some have called the "degaying" of the epidemic that occurred within our own ranks. It became a source of divisiveness and despair among AIDS activists. The movement itself would diminish gay sexuality, first in the name of political efficacy, then in the name of inclusiveness for other forgotten peoples with AIDS, and perhaps always out of a discomfort, even among gay men, with the disordering sexual wildness in gay men that was deemed to have spurred the epidemic in the first place. When an ACT UP flyer in 1991 noted that eleven thousand "women, children, and men" had died of AIDS so far that year, the ranking seemed suspiciously reminiscent of degrees of putative innocence. These particular activists were too callous or callow to include the Stonewall movement itself among their progenitors: an ACT UP outreach broadside called forth the "activist tradition of the civil rights and women's movements and groups like the Young Lords," omitting any reference to the activist roots in the gay movement of most ACT UP members. AIDS activism partnered with the virus in eradicating homosexual history.

Finally, Michael Callen, one of the founders of the PWA movement, called the bluff. "If I hear one more time that AIDS is not a gay disease, I shall vomit. Most of what has been noble about America's response to AIDS has been the direct result of the lesbian and gay community," Callen declared in a March 1989 article in New York's PWA Coalition *Newsline*. "All this AIDS-is-not-a-gay-disease hysteria is an insulting attempt to downplay the contributions of lesbians and gay men."

Just as infants with AIDS became repositories for public sympathy, the deadly swath HIV has cut among the nation's artists lent itself to noncontroversial sentimentality. December 1 was designated World AIDS Day by the World Health Organization, and has long been commemorated by "A Day without Art." Museums drape paintings in black to symbolize art never made or completed because the life of an artist was cut short; at night, the White House and all the beacons of Western capitalism on the New York skyline dim their floodlights. The fact that the great majority of dead artists were also gay men is made to seem irrelevant, even though it's the reason *why* they are dead. And the Names Project, its quilt panels spread out over dozens of acres, is probably the largest cruising ground ever created, though the beautiful gay men who are its objects of desire are all dead. It is not a bed of sex or loss, however; instead, in the eyes of its media team, it is one huge innocent-baby blanket, marketed to stir sentiment and not the grievous fury that arises from impossible desire.

For a time in the late 1980s, the ACT UP media committee met at Vito Russo's apartment, filling the rooms with young, energetic activists who fell all over themselves with ideas for bringing attention to the epidemic and hope to themselves. Yet Vito once expressed an appalling loneliness to me, not because he lacked company or a cause, but because he was bereft of the community he had helped to create and the friendships and connections and personal history that went with it. It was a kind of loneliness for which there was no remedy or cure. And it was a loneliness not just existential but social and political — the fierce solitude of the last soldier left standing.

In the late 1980s, gay activism took hold around the AIDS issue, and in forums like ACT UP, AIDS activism became the cusp where the two generations met. The Stonewall activists had knowledge and experience but were enervated by the incredible toll of sickness and death; the new, AIDS generation was crackling with the explosive force of young people expanding their lives by embracing identity as gay men and lesbians. But the gap between those two generations was not ever bridged, even by activism.

"Prior to the AIDS crisis, there wasn't much talent in the gay rights movement," Michelangelo Signorile wrote in the *Advocate*. "The gay movement had only . . . those people who simply weren't good enough to make it in the real world. But the AIDS crisis suddenly sucked in talent: stockbrokers, television producers, artists, writers, and businesspeople." This statement is a reprehensibly inaccurate portrait of the gay men who built the community institutions that awaited Signorile when he left his own closet in the early 1980s. It is also a rather appalling fetishization of white-collar professionals. Few comments so abjectly express the separation between the two generations, the ahistorical attitude of younger men barreling into the gay community, the triumph of middle-class assimilationist notions that have come to dominate mainstream gay thought, and the perhaps inevitable process of sons disinheriting themselves from their desiccated fathers.

As those with a cultural awareness of the antiwar or civil rights movements know, young people who came of age in the 1960s were exposed to social values that often led the brightest and most talented of all classes to reject "career tracks" in favor of social activism; the meaning of work lay not in high salaries or status, but in the degree of personal satisfaction it might provide. Those women and men whom Signorile perceived as not "good enough to make it in the real world" possessed the conviction and self-esteem necessary to reject one of the most profound taboos in history. In a scant ten years, men like Michael Lynch and Vito Russo had created a movement with thousands of organizations and activities. How can they not be called heroes?

As AIDS exhaustion set in after 1992, shunning AIDS in favor of issues such as gays in the military and spousal rights was an attempt by the newer generation to thrust aside the yoke of a plague; to cease identifying their sexuality with the struggle against the stigma of epidemic, to break the ancient bond between the homosexual and disease, just as assimilationists in the 1970s sought to sever the link between the homosexual and the criminal.

Young gay people, newly emerged and HIV-negative, ached to make their own mark. By 1990, ACT UP had spun off another organization, Queer Nation, and a new, militant identity politics arose, "on the discredited ruins of the old gay movement," as the writer David Leavitt glibly phrased it, having made himself an expert on AIDS activism by attending several ACT UP meetings and then writing about them for the *New York Times Magazine*. His comment added an odd, vaguely antagonistic and Oedipal tone to the revisionist history it implied. Young gay men sometimes complained that the Stonewall generation of Vito Russo and Michael Lynch had "ruined it" for them through sexual profligacy, destroying further opportunity to indulge in the same sexual possibilities their forebears had. There is no logic to this. Their version of the 1970s offered in public debate is usually silent on so much that defined the times beyond sex acts: Anita Bryant; the Briggs Initiative; the assassination of San Francisco's first gay supervisor, Harvey Milk, and the riots after his killer was convicted merely of manslaughter; obscenity charges against gay newspapers; the fury in response to the murders of gay men at the Ramrod bar at the bottom of Christopher Street; three hundred men rounded up in bathhouse raids and carted off to jail in a single night. In this version of history, featuring hedonism as its only rationale, struggle disappeared. With the premature extinction of so many memories, the battles of the Stonewall generation were willfully forgotten.

So often I had a sense of déjà vu when I observed the activists of the nineties: the Queer Nation kiss-ins that early liberationists called "throat-ramming"; the angry debate over "outing," which even the most radical gay activists once forbade as "closet-busting"; the collective gush when "gay" was on the cover of *Newsweek* in 1994, just as when *Time* had done the same in April 1979; the rise of stars coming out in television or in sports; even the everlasting battles over bathhouse openings and public-sex venues, later to be sponsored by groups like Sex Panic!, whose vocabulary is older than many of its activists. All these things began in the 1970s. The same hot issues, aborted by the advent of AIDS, have been recycled in the 1990s: gays in the military, media representation, bisexuality, sexuality versus intimacy, age-of-consent laws, gay marriage rights, mainstreaming as opposed to ghettoization. The gay liberation perspective of changing the erotophobic nature of society has been replaced by a vision of very civil rights and what the conservative gay writer Bruce Bawer calls "a place at the table," without much questioning the menu, the attitude of the hosts, or who might still go hungry.

What AIDS killed, along with the leadership, was the memory of gay *liberation* as a radical ideology of sexuality and intimacy, and the relationship between an individual and his community. After the deaths of almost two hundred thousand gay men, several apartheids flourish among us. One exists between those who have survived to remember and those too young to remember, or too juvenile to care, about stories of lives before their own. Another occurs between those who are not infected and those who are, men who are further separated into those who might survive and those for whom new drugs will be too little or too late. Infected or not, whether younger or older, when they look to rebuild the house of homosexuality, they do not look to the past for their tools.

Michael Lynch was angry when he discovered he too was HIV-positive, which surprised me. Did he really think such a Fire Island bunny as he might avoid it? He continued to live and teach in Toronto, aching for his occasional long sabbaticals in New York City, where he spent yellowing afternoons searching for the pottery shards left by male-male lovers. In Toronto, he renovated an old Victorian house into two apartments with his lover, Billy Lewis. Billy took the third floor, while Michael lived in a cavernous space created by the first two stories with the floor removed. A stairway, stark as a painting by Giacometti, led past soaring bookcases to the sleeping loft, where he'd had a sink and running water installed in a bedside closet, for cleaning up after sex. He kept his body immaculately muscled, and posed nude for a photographer. He bragged of being the only forty-five-year-old professor of American literature to appear in a centerfold in *Honcho* magazine. He published a small but intense book of poetry called *These Waves of Dying Friends*.

To everyone's surprise, Billy Lewis would die first, in 1987. He'd just earned his Ph.D. in biochemistry and launched his career in AIDS research when a bout of pneumocystis pneumonia demolished the fragile alveoli of his lungs. In a hospital on a respirator, he was injected with paralyzing drugs until he underwent heart failure, two weeks later.

After his diagnosis, Michael faded slowly into air, thinner, grayer, smaller, the color evaporating from his blue eyes and replaced by a haunted sheen. Sometimes in New York I would turn a corner, and Michael, on a visit from Toronto, would be walking toward me. Among half a million people at the 1987 gay march on Washington, we somehow bumped into each other and spent half a day together. "What was the point of all that work, all that writing?" he asked me. "It'll all be wiped away by AIDS."

"It's going to get a lot worse," I said.

He nodded. "A lot worse."

We had both seen statistics, where a few tens of thousands of dead gay men would, in only a few years, become hundreds of thousands. With such numbers, it seemed impossible for either of us to escape. Yet if Michael didn't hold a lot of hope for his own immediate prospects or those of his friends, he had to know that he had been part of a larger change, one that would more subtly alter the notions of sex, dissimulation, and shame we all had lived with for so long. On another occasion, Michael told me this story:

His son Stefan spent the winters with his mother in San Francisco and the summers with his father in Toronto. He had lived among lesbians and gay men since preschool, and as a prepubescent had used the word *straight* as a pejorative. One May, fourteen-year-old Stefan prepared to fly north. His mother phoned Michael and mentioned that their son had something to tell him. A few days later, Michael and Stefan were together in Toronto. For a moment, Stefan stammered, and hemmed and hawed. Then, almost with embarrassment, he came out to his beloved father. As a heterosexual.

"It's like having an extension of yourself instead of an opposite." Those words were uttered by a heterosexual teenager who had experimented with gay sex, and perhaps his naiveté discloses a clue to the real nature of homosexual difference. It suggests that an erotic attraction to a member of the same sex is only a manifestation of personality traits that are programmed into some people on a more profound level of awareness. There need be nothing mystical or essentialist about the notion of a gay sensibility, or gay difference, if it is posited as the awareness of a class of men who had similar experiences growing up, and share a common behavior now. The seed of identity is the individual, but it grows in the soil of shared experience. The dichotomy of assimilation or difference, social construction or essentialism, could just as well be framed in the more appropriately American way of "assimilation *and* difference." Is it possible to construct a social identity that genuinely values that formulation?

If gay men and lesbians are to assimilate and still retain what makes them extraordinary, challenging, difficult, and enlivened, it can only be in a society constructed very differently from this one. Increasingly, left-wing theorists accuse identity politics of divisiveness, blaming it for fragmenting progressive movements for social change, and declare that what is needed is a politics that transcends gender. This harks back to an old chestnut from the 1960s: that the "revolution" is indivisible. Yet it seems that gay men have a special place in the phalanx of social change: eradicating the erotophobic nature of Western culture.

Arguably, the modern gay movement is already steering society away from the punitive and prejudicial Judeo-Christian model. The role of the berdache in Native American cultures offers a model for the integration of homosexual behavior into American culture. Berdaches dressed and lived as women and had a highly valued priestly or shamanistic function in their tribes. Anthropologist Walter Williams points out that a berdache was not the same as a "gay man," but closer to a subset of the modern gay community, men who are called queens or drag queens. Native societies integrated their "difference" by creating a socially useful function for them. This model remains imperfect, however, because it excludes masculine-identified gay men. Homosexual Indians today often prefer to be called gay instead of berdache — not to assimilate into white culture, but because the modern category "gay" has expanded the range of possibility for homosexual men. A berdache was expected to be the passive partner in sex, because native cultures organized desire into passive and active roles that corresponded to female and male gender categories. Being "gay" has no such restrictions.

In its erotophilic vision, gay liberation presents itself as a movement for everyone, not just those who prefer same-sex partners. It can be argued that the greatest contribution the category "gay" has made to models of human desire in modern times is that it allows an individual to change from passive to active or vice versa, depending on the partner, the position, or the desire of the moment. In a way that is free of the baggage borne by their heterosexual counterparts, gay men and lesbians present all of us with the idea that power is something that is not mongered; it can instead be willingly assumed by one partner and accepted by another. This calls for an acceptance of what Michael Bronski calls "the role which pleasure must play in all aspects of our lives." There is clearly a long distance to go. And the wounds caused by AIDS to the idea of gay liberation will not be healed for at least a generation.

On his last Gay Pride Day, in 1990, Vito Russo sat on the third-floor balcony of Larry Kramer's apartment at Fifth Avenue and Washington Square North. He was drawn and weary from the ruthless toll of chemotherapy, but it was a perfect vantage to watch the parade, five hours long and a few hundred thousand strong, wind its way downtown and through the Village. As the ACT UP contingent, in ranks three blocks long, reached that corner, heads turned up to spot Vito, hands began to wave in salute, and deafening shouts of "Vito! We love you, Vito!" rose. The contingent strode past, the cheer growing in decibels from rank to rank. As Vito stood on the balcony like a potentate receiving the martial accolades of troops, his face opened to a kind of baffled joy and he wept. Joy for what was, sorrow for all that was lost.

When the activists of the Stonewall generation began to die, they offered their torch to another generation of young gay men. This is their great triumph and precisely what gay communities owe to fallen heroes: after a century of failed attempts to emancipate homosexuals, despite a virus's holocaust, the gay liberation movement that evolved from the Stonewall riots propelled those ideas into a new and equally dangerous era with its dying strength. These successors have their own task: to create an erotophilic society with an ethics of the body that would include the right to speech and thought, the right to reproductive and sexual decision-making, freedom from torture and the death penalty, the right to health care, and the right to euthanasia.

Gay identity may be transient, limited by culture, epoch, and the immense affluence Western societies enjoy. But it is also a common shelter for high mountain travelers, on a path leading to a world that values pleasure and diversity. When Michael Lynch and his fellow historians began to reconstruct a narrative of same-sex behavior in history, they found men who were like modern homosexuals, and yet not. But what unites those men with the present is Eros, the history of love and pleasure in human life, of intimacy, of bonds, great friendships, fraternal love, the dear love of comrades.

To Michael Lynch, the poet's image — brothers like two stone towers, side by side and solid in the flowing river — was a parable for the choices offered to gay men for their intimate relationships. It is not the tyranny of a suspect monogamy based on the inherent inequality between men and women, but the myth of brothers — independence and difference bonded by affection and Eros. A eulogist made this point at Michael's memorial in 1991: Michael believed this could also be the foundation of peace among all men. Like other young men and women of his generation, and perhaps like enough of the next, he wanted to make love instead of war.

7

Beyond the Culture of Love

THE FATE OF GAY BROTHERHOOD

Q UERIBUS. PERYPETEUSE. PADERN. Durban. Aguillar. These ancient names roll out from memory like a song.

In the south of France there is a range of mountains called the Corbières, and on five of its windswept peaks stand withering stone ruins of walls, towers, ramparts, and battlements. A thousand years ago, castles were built there, leagues apart and high, to defend a people threatened with invasion. From these heights, enemies might be seen, even at a great distance.

The faltering stones behold the valley of Roussillon. To the east the curdled waters of the Mediterranean glitter, turquoise in summer, lavender at sunset, in winter the color of lead. Across the sprawling valley far to the south are the mountains of the Pyrenees, like tidal waves frozen in a swell, the highest one the snow-capped peak of Canigou. On the other side is Spain. Below, in the valley, the French city of Perpignan.

Sometime through the centuries, these fortresses became known as the Five Brothers: Queribus, Perypeteuse, Padern, Durban, Aguillar — all stone remnants of the enigmatic people known to us as the Cathars. In the eleventh and twelfth centuries, their civilization flourished as a center of learning and the arts in that part of France called Languedoc.

In 1208, Pope Innocent III branded Cathar religious doctrine "the Albigensian heresy," after the city of Albi, and summoned a crusade. Louis IX of France craved the lands of Languedoc. He unleashed his general, Simon de Montfort, and the Cathars were slaughtered, pretty much to the last child, and their cathedrals and universities razed.

But while their civilization has been extinct for almost a thousand years, a certain Cathar legacy lives on, indeed has blossomed in our own spiritually impoverished time. It is this: the modern cult of romantic love.

We live in a culture saturated with love. In contemporary Western culture it is a central obsession. We yearn for it to come into our lives. When it does, we believe that it transforms us, for a while.

The notion of true love is inescapable in music, literature, film, theater. It seems a reason to go on living, as vital as breath or babies. For heterosexual teenagers, the lyrics of popular music work as a kind of how-to course, socializing them throughout their adolescence in the nature of romance and the protocols of contemporary courtly love. The lyrics of modern popular songs show that while male singers predominantly celebrate falling in love, female singers are more likely to sing about lost love.

Whether we're in love, ache for love, or bemoan its loss, no one among us likes to be told that romantic love is not as natural, instinctual, and God-given as, say, heterosexuality; that it is, like heterosexuality, a construct, an invention of culture, and a fairly recent one at that. A thousand years ago, romantic love was a kind of madness that overcame people; to be wounded by one of Cupid's arrows was not a stroke of good fortune. Asian cultures have treated it with disdain. Revolutionary cultures have suppressed it. When a Cape Breton Island choir made plans to tour communist China in the 1970s, they were instructed to excise from their repertoire all songs about love.

At the turn of the last millennium, when women were little more than the chattel of men, romantic love represented an act of rebellion. As it evolved over the centuries in European myth, the cult of love helped to break down the prevailing system of marriages that were engineered for dynastic and economic reasons. Romantic love was the basis for a new morality emerging from the Middle Ages and ripening into the twentieth century, an ethos that exonerated disobedience before the father, justified a woman's act of independence, and encouraged her to value her body and its desires.

In the history of familial forms, romance has little prominence until our own time, when the myth of perfect love has worked as cement to patch the entire shaky edifice of modern marriage. In the Victorian age, the idea of romantic love began to merge with the institution of marriage, even as the age stripped women of the possibility of carnal desire. Love rationalized copulation as a burden to be shouldered dutifully for the Empire. The feminist Shulamith Firestone has written that romantic love is a device used in a patriarchal and sexist society to raise a woman up from her lower caste and place her on a pedestal, thus enabling a man to love what would otherwise be beneath him. The object on the pedestal is a fantasy, perhaps calculated to disappoint. The price paid by the female for such veneration can prove morbidly high: the dissolution of her identity and the validation of her life through his.

As the twentieth century began, erotic passion was restored to romantic love, and once again, until the 1960s, it became the moral rationalization that permitted men and women sexual freedom before marriage. But "true love" also implies a lifelong commitment to one person. The contemporary cult of romantic love remains the foundation on which the ideology of lifetime heterosexual monogamy is built. The cult is strengthened by the demands placed on modern marriage, an institution that the German sexologist Gunter Schmidt calls "compensatory." He writes that sexuality "is supposed to hold marriages and relationships together because they scarcely fulfill material functions any longer; it is supposed to promote self-realization and self-esteem in a society that makes it more and more difficult to feel . . . worth something. . . . It is supposed to drive out coldness and powerlessness. . . . All discontent — political, social, and personal — is meant to be deflected into the . . . relationship sector in order to be compensated."

Monogamy's opposite, promiscuity, has recently served to separate in the public mind the "innocent" victims of HIV from the ones judged to be the instigators of their own disease. But in the decade after Stonewall and before AIDS, the myriad activities grouped under the rubric of promiscuity were enormously varied and complex in practice. Promiscuity was only the most visible manifestation of a grand experiment in developing new kinds of relationships in a world that, to many young people in the sixties and seventies, was rife with bad ones.

The AIDS crisis destroyed this particular endeavor of gay liberation by engendering a quick retreat to the ideal of the monogamous couple. Love gave life easy meaning, and commitment equaled safety. As people gay or straight, we have not paid much attention to the concept of love or how we use it; we have retreated to a cave most of us have not lifted our lamps to examine very carefully. A fear of plague has bequeathed us — whatever our sexual orientation — a paucity of meaning to bring to the lovers in our lives.

The first time I visited my friend Gilles in Perpignan, I demanded to see the *châteaux cathares,* and he told me about the Five Brothers in the Corbières. Gilles was a schoolteacher who taught in a small village outside Perpignan, where he lived upstairs in a sixteenth-century building that housed the school and the town hall. One day in his little village, I watched a funeral procession wind its way through the cobbled street. In front of the church, the villagers — farmers and tradesmen — stopped and waited while half a dozen men carried the coffin inside. The service was broadcast outside on loudspeakers, not because the sanctuary was full, but because most of the mourners refused to enter a Catholic church. The Roman pope might consider them his flock, but they certainly did not acknowledge him as pope. Like many other people who had grown up in the region, Gilles considered himself *un vrai Cathare*, almost a thousand years after the fact.

Gilles took me first to Queribus, a tiny castle, almost intact at the summit of a bald stony mountain. Thick stone walls surrounded a strange octagonal keep with a high Gothic window on one side that faced the sun at summer's solstice. We climbed a narrow rocky path on a chilly November day. The path turned into stone steps, hugging a wall and spiraling upward toward a portcullis. An icy wind blowing across the valley of Roussillon tugged at our hats and coats, sometimes turned about in sudden blasts that threatened to bowl us over the edge. It howled through the gashes in the crumbling outer wall, gaping stone doors and windows. We almost had to shout to speak to each other.

Gilles burst into a yodeling song, his voice trilling off a line of what seemed nonsense sounds, perfect syllables that carried through the windstorm. A smile of pure pleasure shaped his face. Later, he explained to me that the yodeling song was part of a secret language developed during the Cathars' exile in the mountains. After the annihilation of their civilization, as the Cathars hid among these peaks, they shouted their words across chasms, down ravines, from cliff to cliff, and through the wind's scream. Their cries were words in code that had no meaning to any eavesdropping enemy. Today, people know the songs by rote, but like the Cathar texts of love, it is said their true meaning is lost to history, buried under centuries of the victors' debris.

Catharism grew out of an extraordinary confluence of religious philosophies. Manichaeism, a third-century Persian religion, traveled through the Balkans and across the Alps into southern France, where it provided people with the seeds of a new theology. Christianity was weak in the south of France, and Moorish learning, at the height of its accomplishments, spread north from Spain across the Pyrenees. These currents of faith mingled in Provence and Languedoc. They begot the Church of Love — AMOR, as opposed to ROMA, the Church of Rome, to which the Cathars were implacably opposed.

Christianity posits human beings as creatures who have fallen from grace, separated from God by what Kierkegaard called an "infinite qualitative difference." In opposition, Cathars believed that human beings *are* God, each one a part of the universal soul separated by the sin of birth and earthly existence. Life was a journey that took the Cathar back to his true state of divine being in death. This doctrine of immanence gave the Cathars an attitude toward life that could be either ascetic or robust. Women as well as men were allowed to be "elect" or priestly; abortion was permitted and war absolutely forbidden. Giving birth was a sin, however necessary, because becoming embodied separated a divine being from the universal godhead. Thus the pleasures of sex were considered differently than the duties of procreation. While Catharism is more popularly known for its asceticism, one of its bishops proclaimed that there existed "no sin below the navel."

Troubadours, musicians who traveled in pairs throughout medieval Europe, arose from the Cathars' civilization. The lyrics of their songs addressed a beloved as "my lord," or "my lady," a form of verse borrowed from the unabashedly sexual poetry of the Sufis, an Islamic sect founded by mystics in the ninth century. For Cathar troubadours, their songs of a lover who yearned to be with the beloved were a symbolic expression of the Cathar doctrine that the act of death reunited the individual with the godhead. This was also the theme of romantic legends that grew from Cathar culture and spread across Europe, tales of star-crossed romances that ended in the deaths of both lovers — which was not an end of love, but an ultimate reunification in God.

After the Cathars were branded heretics, the pope called on King Louis IX of France for a crusade against them. The important Cathar fortress of Montségur, supposedly impregnable, fell to Simon de Montfort in 1237, after a nine-month siege. When his soldiers asked which of the sixty thousand human beings inside the castle should be slain and which spared, the venerable general cried, "Kill them all! Let God decide!"

The Five Brothers held out for a dozen more years. Queribus was the last to fall. By 1248 it was all over: King Louis added Languedoc to his kingdom and was beatified by the pope, who, buoyed by the genocide of the Cathars, launched the Roman Church on successive crusades to Palestine.

De Montfort's infamous exhortation to "kill them all" has survived centuries to seep into the present. It can been seen today on T-shirts in the store windows around Fort Bragg in North Carolina. Catharist symbolism and imagery also had permeated European culture too deeply and for too long to be eradicated by the Albigensian crusade. The legends and poetry remained — no longer as sources of spiritual sustenance connecting humans to the godhead and venerating death, but as the yearning texts of romantic love. The cult grew over centuries, and acquired power until our own secular age, where it has come to fulfill the existential need for ecstasy and despair, for connection to the greater whole, that the Christian religion once did. The passion of *Tristan and Isolde* is the archetype, *Romeo and Juliet* the history, and *West Side Story* the result. In *Against Interpretation*, Susan Sontag has written that our obsession with love "expresses the central and peculiarly modern preoccupation of the loss of feeling. . . . It is the main way in which we test ourselves for strength of feeling and find ourselves deficient."

In 1992, a lesbian serial killer in Florida was sentenced to death for killing middle-aged white heterosexual men, all of whom, she claimed, had sexually attacked her first. During the same week in Milwaukee a court convicted Jeffrey Dahmer, a deranged gay man desperate for love and terrified of abandonment, who consummated his desire for companionship by eating his victims' hearts.

Each of these stories might be an allegory of fear and desire in our own erotic lives, extremes in madness of what everyone has felt: love and hate, approach and avoidance, attraction and repulsion, or moments of transcendence that, over time, turn to bone. Each of these murderers, however macabre their acts, acted within a range of narratives specific to the context: *he made me do it*, a justification for the rage and robbery that followed; *I want to be a part of you so you'll never leave* — a kind of gastronomical consummation of longing to be one with the beloved.

A portent of Dahmer's crime appears in an essay by Danish feminist Suzanne Brøgger attacking monogamy, which is essential to the idea of romantic love, as "institutionalized cannibalism." In "Monogamy: The Cannibalism of Our Time," published in a book called *Deliver Us from Love*, Brøgger writes: "In our culture, every one of us, in the course of our lives, has the right to eat at least one other person, provided only that we eat every last morsel and not just nibble." Or leave crumbs.

All our adult relationships — professional, collegial, amicable, and romantic — contribute to the development of our personality, but only in the sphere of love and sex does our culture demand we get *everything* from just one person. For the millions of people whose country of birth is a remote behemoth of faint allegiances, whose society is church socials and bridge parties, whose livelihood constitutes a series of workplace games that lack humanistic content; for the millions of married men, and women, who find themselves bereft of other intimate companions; for those innumerable parents whose children puzzle and secretly disappoint them by their differentness — for all these, for most of us, the only true community is the nation of two that is romantic, or at least marital, love.

But perfect stasis in our world is quite rare, which is why the movies end as lovers ride off into sunsets, not with them arguing over washing-machine payments. Love is there as long as your back is turned; the moment you look at it, it morphs into something far more complicated and less namable. What creates the great romances of history is not what brings lovers together, but what tears them apart. The myth of doomed or unhappy love began when the Cathar-influenced legends and the songs of the troubadours were taken literally, instead of as metaphors for a longing to leave the mortal coil and be in God.

Over the centuries, the stories of lovers who were reunited only in death spawned variations, such as the modern fascination with unrequited love. Tristan and Isolde's frustrated and fatal ardor gave way to *Gone with the Wind*'s angst-filled treadmill: when he's ready, she's not; when Scarlett has finally come to her senses, Rhett doesn't give a damn.

On the surface such dramas may involve strong-willed women, but inevitably, when love is lost it is a punishment for overreaching. The stories of Lady Caroline Lamb's love for the callous Lord Byron, and Susan Hayward in *Backstreet*, come immediately to mind. Here, love is doomed to hopelessness. It is the love of the martyr, and martyrdom at the altar of love. It means: *she died of a broken heart*. We are, as Alfred Chester wrote in *Ismael*, "destined never to profoundly have whom we love nor to profoundly love whom we have . . . contemptuous of those who are foolish enough to love us, adoring of those who find us unworthy." Susan Sontag has proposed that we value romantic love not for the possibilities of

joy it may bring, but for the promise of pain: "The sensibility we
have inherited identifies spirituality and seriousness with turbu-
lence, suffering and passion . . . it has been spiritually fashionable
to be in pain. Thus it is not love that we overvalue, but suffering —
more precisely the spiritual merits and benefits of suffering."

If we value love because of a deeply inculcated need to suffer, or
play the martyr, a potential partner may trigger a romantic response
not because he is "made" for us, but precisely because he's the one
with whom we are totally incompatible, someone who can unleash
a host of masochistic desires and emotions; someone who, in fact,
has all the right personality traits to ensure it won't work out. Is an
affair rooted in romantic love a recipe for codependency, a partner-
ship in which two people play out a psychodrama programmed in
childhood by the warped experiences of intimacy amid the endless
dysfunctions of nuclear families?

Such dynamics, according to Sontag, are "an extension of the
spirit of Christianity," contrary to the assertion of the famous French
historian Denis De Rougement, who labels romantic love a Cathar
heresy subverting Western civilization. What De Rougement ignored were the effects of medieval Catholicism on the Cathars'
ideas after their annihilation, when the troubadour's poetic language entered macabre centuries of inquisitions and the black
death. Cathar poetry, exalting love of my lord or lady, was taken up
by Christian mystics who advocated a scourging asceticism and
long nights of the soul as the path to God. The remnants of carnal
passion that had once suffused Cathar ideas lingered behind a
screen of politically correct religiosity. European paintings began
to show Christian martyrs undergoing a panoply of devious tortures
devised by the minds of men, but with their faces suffused with
erotic ecstasy, indeed, orgasm. It was such a pleasure to die for
Christ. Suffering became the hallmark of spiritual pursuit. Poetry
that had expressed a desire for union in the One became instead

the language of self-punishment, and a celebration of a longing for completion that can both destroy and vivify us.

Emerging from the context of the women's movement, the first post-Stonewall gay male liberationists realized that relationships with other men had the potential to be different from — and possibly better than — the bonds between men and women. Two gay men could come to each other as lovers with mutual gender equality, in contrast to the inherently unequal status between a man and a woman. This project to define new relationships between men linked the Stonewall movement to the earliest years of modern gay identity, when Walt Whitman explored ideas of "adhesiveness" and Edward Carpenter wrote of the "dear love of comrades." And in our own time, William Burroughs has suggested that relationships among men are based less on romantic love than on what he has called "recognition."

Gay men began to create a new ideology of relationships; new ways of thinking about sex, romance, and commitment became part of some lives. Love could be a multiplicity instead of exclusivity; commitment could be different to different people; each relationship could be mutually defined by the partners, starting at square one. And each bond could be entirely different from other relationships in the life of each partner.

The models created by gay men include having primary and secondary relationships, third-person and bisexual commitments, fathering arrangements, and long-distance or intermittent affairs between two men. Fundamentally, these attempts question the cultural linkage between the three elements that make up our concept of romantic love: passionate emotions, good sex, and economic commitment. It apportioned them in different ways. These models can be traced back to the Bloomsbury circle in London in the 1920s, and New York modernists. Gay men began to popularize living and sexual arrangements that had once been options only for the privileged or the bohemian. With the status of women changing rapidly, and enormous confusion entering heterosexual relationships, the structures gay men created to meet family and sexual needs were envied, and sometimes adopted, by heterosexual women and men who were charting their own way into unexplored territory.

Stereotypes exist of the lonely older gay man, spurned by a subculture that values youth and beauty. When a gay man comes out to his parents, this specter is often their greatest fear for their son's future. Yet many gay men who remain single claim a network of close, supportive friendships that echo and enlarge the heterosexual context of marriage, children, and grandchildren.

Now, in the 1980s and 1990s, waves of mass death have eradicated these networks, letting them fall silent, man by man by man. For years on Gay Pride Day in New York I marched with ten men, who disappeared one by one over the next decade like little Indians. Only I remained alive. At Fire Island Pines, certain beach houses are famous for having sheltered a now-vanished clan, eight men or ten or twelve who all disappeared from the face of the earth in the period of a few years.

To epidemiologists this is a *cluster*, and one of the earliest — some forty-three gay men in Los Angeles — led them to the infamous Patient Zero. In the human world, the scientific precision of a cluster becomes a cruel abstraction, drowning out the myriad small familied groups of men whose real relationships were complex, caring, contradictory, and compassionate. The clan within the tribe. The kith without the kin. The fraternity built of lovers and friends, their bonds animated by desires they have no language to express, with no code they can offer to the outside world, gay or straight, to affirm the truth they live.

Single heterosexuals have also suffered this loss. "I don't want to be the last apple on the tree," my friend Josie told me. She is a friend from my youth in Canada. Josie meant that when her gay brother dies and all her other gay friends too, she's going to be the only one left. Josie is single and in her forties. Twenty years ago, in college, she had a chance at marital bliss with a man she loved deeply. She found herself pregnant and chose to abort. It was a turning point, for both of them, to turn elsewhere.

She was telling me how last year she had traveled to the same remote provincial city for a reunion with that man, and they talked about their diverged paths. If she'd carried the baby, her old boy-friend would have left architecture school to marry her, getting a job to support his family. Just as his father had done several decades earlier. "And we would've had a relationship exactly like my parents," he concluded, remembering years growing up with his father's bitterness, his mother trapped.

Josie moved to the Big City, and her college lover finished school, married, had children, stayed in the town he grew up in. When Josie went back to visit, she found that a certain love for him abides, but twenty years had also made a difference between the one who had stayed and the one who left.

"We've lost more people than they've met in their entire lives!" Josie concluded, summing up the intersection of personal history and cataclysm.

At one time it was the psychotherapist's task to help a lonely and isolated patient acquire the capacity to enter into a healthy romantic relationship. That approach assumed that the patient desired such a relationship and could not be psychically or socially complete without one. Today, increasingly, the goal is for clients to lead fulfilling lives as single people. This is true not only for gay men and lesbians who have found themselves unwilling to adhere to the old forms: more and more, professional women are deciding to live independently, even to rear children on their own. Divorced people must do the same, if not quite by choice. All people who find themselves living lives independent of a single lover must confront the basic human questions of defining and managing intimacy and desire. For many of us, living singly among a community of friends may be a more realistic and satisfying achievement than yearning for a kind of coupledom that is unobtainable.

A pervasive, unspoken — and very normal — problem among heterosexual couples is the sexual boredom than can set in after several years of marriage. Many gay male couples, including those whose lives and spirits you couldn't separate with a crowbar, attempt to solve this problem by having a long-term, committed primary relationship that is sexually open, and that sometimes leads to secondary romantic or sexually passionate affairs. Often these relationships transcend sexual jealousy. The first bond might be a lifelong commitment, and with it perhaps a mortgage, or joint artistic or professional careers. The second might be the torrid or tormented romantic dalliance outside it. Another relationship might be with a previous lover, the two men bound by history and mutual care. Or the bond could be with a lover who lived far away and had infrequent visits. Men who meet as one-night stands might end up buying adjoining apartments; men who begin as housemates might end up lovers. One longed-for relationship among single gay men is with a "sex buddy," a bond with another man when both are driven by enormous chemical attraction but have absolutely nothing else in common. They may not even see each other frequently. I know of such relationships that have lasted years and are warm, affectionate, and animating.

No one would claim that such experiments didn't reveal new and different relationship problems. Wrestling to find a balance between intimacy and sexual play is a problem unique to our times. In a short story, Alfred Chester summed it this way: "In the equation of love, no plus can exist except by virtue of a minus." Gay men may share an inherently equal gender status, unlike heterosexual men and women, but there are other imbalances men sometimes seek out: the differences in youth and age, in class, among what Andrew Holleran has called the "democracy of beauty." For AIDS, gay liberationists in San Francisco began to develop a dialogue about man-on-man sexism, one that recognized and addressed inherent disparities underlying the assumption of gender equality. But in the chaos of these embryonic new forms there existed the promise that arising and thriving among us could be new promises of love.

Once the bogeyman that HIV represented had made its impact, the gay community retreated instantly from the idea of sexual positivism, its most uncertain and exciting turf. Closing bathhouses was only part of it; urging gay men to "relate" in a meaningful romantic relationship, as the *Advocate* urged as early as 1984, represented another. Gay men were telling other gay men to shut down most of their points of entry and not to be penetrated with possibility.

Gay men expect themselves to be "coupled" more today than they were ten or fifteen years ago, yet many seem to be very nervous about what they think they long for. Enormous time and emotional energy are expended in a quest for a lifelong partner. In spite of what Quentin Crisp has told us, that "there is no great dark man," finding the one right romantic partner has become the all-consuming quest of homosexual existence. Gay culture is built not around sex but around the longing for one true love. Love is always as close as two songs away on the radio, two men away on the dance floor. The increasing commercialization of gay sex in the last two decades has presented dating and sex play only as entertaining and desperate methods through which a gay man seeks his one true Man-Grail. Of course, just like straight people, gay men start out with little idea of why they want a man or what they would do with him once they got him. They just want to feel warmer at night and believe themselves no longer marginalized in the culture of love. Once some facsimile of our desires comes along, we are all thumbs, clumsy with infatuation. We start seeing relationship counsels within weeks of dating, and before moving in. Many of us engage in the psychodramas of the pseudomonogamous couple, where silences are more important than words.

Romantic love is where the myth of happiness in marriage, a.k.a. "domestic bliss," begins. Yet the legal right to plunge into marriage on the heterosexual model is at the top of the post-AIDS gay rights agenda. Love *und* "marriage" was trotted out as shelter from the viral storm. The romantic paradigm was sanctified as a public health measure. Romantic love was appropriated as a miraculous shield, a kind of purity that would protect lovers from the virus. The cult of romantic love serves a metaphysical function, transporting favored individuals to a preternatural zone in which muttered blessings give inviolable protection against a deadly virus, and invisible spirits heal. Of course, HIV sleeps in the marriage bed; it is just ignored there.

In an age where the unconsidered notions of love and marriage have so infected gay men, is it still possible to reach for relationships that can promise more true connection, more life?

Brotherly love. Fraternal love.

Instead of false love, or wasted love, love dreamed of or yearned for, star-crossed or unrequited, troubled or bored love, we could have this: brothers, bound without blood, encountering the vicissitudes of life and time like the stone towers of the Brooklyn Bridge standing side by side and stalwart in the river. Like Gilles's five mountains. Bound through our sex together and our histories, suffused with anger and ever-transforming desire, planted in different landscapes but fed by the same underground streams, we could find in fraternal love a paradigm we might healthily embrace. Recognition. The dear love of comrades.

Yet even the fraternal bond must be quarried anew, because the portrait offered by myth and history is problematic. Osiris and Set; Cain and Abel; Jacob and Esau; the Lion King and his brother;

Querelle and his brother: these are the troublesome doppelgängers of myth, the sexual seducer, the murderer, the fraud, the usurper, the tempter — a crude transmogrification of brotherly love into conflict between good and evil. In at least some of those pairs, one brother is homosexual: Seth, the "effeminate one"; glabrous Jacob — "buffed," in today's parlance — versus hirsute Esau; Cain and Abel, who act out a drama of dominance and submission, culminating in Abel's murder. So that these brothers may receive each other's love, Jean Genet would have them bonded for eternity in guilt and death, the ghost of the beautiful young man forever haunting the cage of his murderer. In Genet's novel *Querelle of Brest*, Querelle the homosexual is concatenated with his brother, the incorruptibly heterosexual Jean. Only by reaching further back in history, to the genesis of civilization, can we go beyond the image of brother hating brother, and begin to see that these are bastardizations of a profound ontology that can magnetize our desires.

In the early kingdoms of ancient Egypt, Osiris's homosexual brother Set was the Divine Troubler, the spirit of disorder, which meant not chaos but the animating energy needed to create its opposite, order. In Set's earthly contendings against his nephew Horus, the son of Osiris and the symbol of spiritual transcendence, Set seduces Horus. In standard interpretations of their great battle, Set rips out Horus's eye, while Horus tears off Set's testicles; this allegory is about the struggle between man's spiritual nature, represented by the eye, the light-receiving organ, and our animal nature, symbolized by testicles.

In this myth from the childhood of our species, carnality is opposed to spirituality, an obstacle to transcendence. While one civilization laid it on the shoulders of a male homosexual god, the ancient Hebrews placed the blame on Eve, the first female. We can trace the influence of ancient myth in our daily lives by comparing two versions of what happened before the Fall in the Garden of Eden. In Genesis, Adam and Eve disobeyed God, and with knowledge, they were ashamed of their naked bodies. In the Gnostic apocrypha, this same couple eats, but with a different result: "they knew that they were naked with regard to knowledge" and were ashamed. But when they saw each other's naked bodies, "they became enamored of one another." We can only surmise the kind of sex-positive, knowledge-loving civilization we might live in had the Gnostic version prevailed over Genesis over the last few thousand years.

Are the fraternal doppelgängers that arise from myth paired opposites who are necessary for competition or conflict? Or are they a way to deny that there are two sexual sides to the male coin? I think Rainer Fassbinder's film version of *Querelle of Brest* — in which the role of Querelle was played by Brad Davis, who later died of AIDS — concerns the modern dialectic between fraternal doppelgängers. At the end, the Madame, her desire for Querelle unrequited, and Querelle's straight brother, the Madame's lover, begin to laugh hysterically.

"*Es gibt keinen Bruder!*" they cry, giddy from the superego's repression of the libido, repeating their words over and over, as if each echo were a little more persuasive. "There is no brother!" is code: it means that homosexuals do not really exist or, if they do, are not human.

The Dutch Egyptologist Te Velde, in his book *The Contendings of Horus and Seth*, has reinterpreted the story as one of erotic and unrequited homosexual love: after sex, when Horus receives Set's semen, he weeps for the loss of Set. Or is Horus, the spirit of transcendence, weeping for the loss of animal love, or perhaps all sensuality of material life that death denies us?

Perhaps this is why the concept of gay marriage is so troublesome to legislators. Like the taboos against same-sex coupling, marriage helps to define what "heterosexual" means; the great fear is of the loss of a characteristic criterion of heterosexual identity.

"They're different animals," as one talking head, referring to homosexual coupling, said on *Nightline*.

As offensive as this comment is, in figurative terms it may be appropriate. Heterosexuality, after all, is not defined by the insertion of a penis into a vagina. Anyone can do that. Heterosexuality is an ideology. The feminist Margaret Small writes that it is

> the basic framework which determines a woman's life. . . . Heterosexual hegemony insures that people think it natural that male and female form a life-long sexual / reproduction unit with the female belonging to the male. . . . Now you go and tell people that there could be another purpose to life, that sexuality can be totally divorced from reproduction, that reproduction could be organized in a totally different way and they'll just laugh and say you're talking about Martians. Heterosexual hegemony insures that people can't even perceive that there could be other possibilities.

There is no brother.

How can men and women have relationships based on mutual equality and independence when cultural love is a paradigm of dominance and submission wherein no plus exists "except by virtue of a minus"? Is romance, the foundation of the ideology of marriage, of the dream of a lifelong partner, beyond redemption? The Cathars believed that every person was equal because every person was divine, and that love should be an expression of longing for the fully realized self. That's a good place to start when trying to love others. Perhaps we should also consider Suzanne Brøgger's conclusion: "I believe that at the moment, our goals with regard to love should be dilettantism, naivete, and superficiality, and that we should strive to achieve them in whatever way we can."

In the first chapter of this book I referred to that vital, spiritually generous victim of the Holocaust, Etty Hillesum. Throughout these pages her brave, tragic presence has haunted me and guided me. While she was awaiting deportation to her death at Auschwitz, Hillesum wrote in a letter: "Why not turn the love that cannot be bestowed on another . . . into a force that benefits the whole community and that might still be love? And if we attempt that transformation, are we not standing on the solid ground of the real world, of reality? A reality as tangible as a bed with a man or a woman in it?"

Romantic love, which goes hand in hand with the dream of marriage, remains the single greatest obsession of our culture, and as a result we are bankrupted by it: we have no other love left to give, either for fellow human beings or for the blue planet we live on. Perhaps in part it is our inability to move beyond searching for love with one other person in a nation of two that has led to the politics of symbols instead of people, and a pornography of death, in which we watch the plight of desperate people on our televisions, and do nothing.

AIDS is a death I'd prefer to these: teenage boys hustled from a Bosnian warehouse to have their throats slit, so the new recruits can have some practice in massacre; a black man in a military uniform, strange fruit hanging from a southern tree; the young gay man shitting his pants after being delivered to his death at the hands of Texas torturers who hate AIDS-ridden faggots; or another young gay man, this one in Wyoming, lured to his own murder by men he hoped could be his friends. As Hannah Arendt told us, in our century it is the good family man who represents the banality of evil. *Homo institutus* and other political somnambulists stamp the requisitions for the various machineries of death. AIDS patients were suffocated between, in one closing hand, the stigma of society and, in the other closing hand, the solipsism of "pure science"; in Bosnia, the West chose not to protect the lives of civilians, mortared in their valley cities exactly like trout shot in a barrel.

Whether it is AIDS or Sarajevo, or Rwanda or Congo, the world's back has grown supple from turning away so often. Between gay men and the tragic people of southeastern Europe there is an older connection, for the Bosnians were also Cathars — or Bogomils, as the Slavs called them; or, as the rest of Europe called them, *Bulgari*, whence the English word *bugger*. In the *Divine Comedy*, Dante places two of the most famous troubadours in Purgatory's Circle of Sodomites. Even the first Sufis were homosexual poets.

Dzevad Karahasan, an eminent Bosnian dramaturge, asks if the Serbs, when they enforced their medieval-style siege of Sarajevo, had not picked up where Simon de Montfort left off. In an essay in the book *Sarajevo: Exodus of a City*, he suggests that an "aesthetic of indifference" is responsible for the pornography of death: "The decision to perceive literally everything as an aesthetic phenomenon — completely sidestepping questions about goodness and the truth — is an artistic decision. . . . [It] started in the realm of art, and went on to become characteristic of the contemporary world." But that perception, uncomfortably astute, might also apply to science without responsibility; the academy without attachment; politics without people; love that lives for form and not content.

I depart from Cathars, from the Christians, and any old religion in which transcendence excludes carnal passion in favor of otherworldly visions. We should begin to focus on the material world we live in, not the one to which we may or may not be going. Clearly, this is no small task, and we need to be reminded that, as journalist Susan Faludi avers, "history is driven . . . by the actions and changing beliefs of large numbers of ordinary people . . . [not] by a few heroic giants who materialize out of nowhere to transform the landscape." Te Velde's reinterpretation of the relationship between Horus and Set suggests to the ordinary person that the spirit might love carnality instead of rejecting it. Each is a gift to the other. Horus, the representation of spirit, weeps for loss of his animal nature.

I would like to see a system of ethics developed from the integrity of each human body and the sanctity of self, instead of calls to "natural law" or "higher moralities." This would be a politics of meaning, at least to me. If the body is inviolable, then human rights extend beyond free speech, free conscience, to freedom in sexual and reproductive decision-making, freedom from being charged with victimless crimes, freedom of access to euthanasia, freedom for every human being to refuse to go to war. Torture would become a form of blasphemy; the death penalty would lose all force of moral suasion. A child would not "belong" to a parent; a child would belong to himself.

Love and death. They are inexplicably linked, and it is precisely at the intersection of the two that AIDS squats, antagonistic to all human love, a lover of death. HIV should be branded an enemy of human love. We should need no other reason as a society to marshal every social resource to eradicate it.

My visits to Gilles almost always followed visits with Hans, yet the love I had for one in no way threatened or competed with the very different feelings I had for the other. Just as both men were individuals, the emotions each conjured in me were distinct and unique. Had I allowed one friendship to overwhelm or eclipse the other, I might never have visited those five chateaus, led by a *vrai Cathare*.

Gilles was a modern troubadour, in a way, not because he sang or wrote love poetry — he did not, he was a teacher — but because, like the troubadours of his ancestral past, he spent his life crisscrossing the distant roads of Europe, east and west. Proud of his twenty-two-centimeter cock, he prowled for sex through the Romania of Ceausescu, cruised Bulgarian truck drivers hauling loads of tomatoes at a rest stop outside Strasbourg.

The last time I visited Gilles, it was a European trip from hell: Hans was sick in Amsterdam, Paris emptied of friends and littered with corpses. In Perpignan, Gilles told me that a month earlier he'd had thrush, his mouth coated with the noxious white yeast. He'd decided to try "aromatherapy" and rigorously followed advice in a book by a diet guru to eat foods that appealed to his sense of smell.

On this visit, we went to Aguillar, a square fortress with round corner towers, less isolated among rolling vineyards than the other four Brothers. There was little left except a floor plan. The inner and outer walls had been razed, the towers little more than stubs poking up from the grassy hillside. Below the outer wall was a Romanesque church, built after the destruction of the Cathars to sanctify heretical ground. It too was a ruin, although the walls and even a part of the brick dome were still standing.

Sometimes, there are words to describe with subtlety what happened next, but this is not one of them: Gilles standing on the remains of the altar with his arms spread wide in the posture of crucifixion, a sweet smile set upon his lips while I knelt in prayer to blow him.

A year after that day, I saw him in New York, when he traveled by car through the American Southwest. In retrospect, I know that he was closing up his life. He said before returning to Europe that it no longer excited him to see new places as it once did; his life, he felt, had turned stale. Maybe that was a deliberately cruel assessment of the world that made his descent into the maw of AIDS a little easier.

We are HIV.

Some months after his trip to New York, I received a short, simple letter from Gilles's sister, stating that Gilles was dead. Today, sometimes, I whisper like a rhyme the names of the five brothers: Queribus, Perypeteuse, Durban, Padern, Aguillar, great fortresses whose ruins endure on the peaks of windswept mountains, guarding forever the green vineyards of Roussillon, the snowcapped Pyrenees, and the glinting waves of the Mediterranean. Gilles and I were never in love, yet for reasons I'm still only partly aware of, his death has been the saddest for me to come to terms with. *Nous étions deux Lycaöns au soleil.*

Sometimes, I hear Gilles whistling the secret language of the mountain people, a language I shall never know. As I shall never share the common, once-promised future with vanished friends and lovers. My future is in ruins; the men I love exist in photographs, a book, a telephone number scrawled on a piece of scrap paper, an old shirt, a beautiful coat. These, and memory, are my companions in the landscape of death.

I think that, like the five mountains, those gay men and I are siblings: Robin, Hans, Vito, Michael, Gilles. In our deaths our ruins remain, and our voices echo. Will our future brothers — our sons — comprehend our words?

ACKNOWLEDGMENTS

Robin Hardy's writing was shaped by the values and ideas of his multitude of friends. After Robin's death, they helped ensure that his voice would be heard.

A great number of Robin's compatriots have died; some of them are memorialized in these pages. Others who are still living deeply influenced his life and his work, among them Louis Albert, Mila Allen, David Baker, Sandy Bernard, Kris Boggild, John Burnside, Olivia Canter, Guillermina Contreras-Arriola, Richard Copeland, Bruce Coville, Robert Croonquist, Martin Delaney, Michael Denneny, Albert Don, Ginny Doran, Andy Fabo, Philip Fotheringham, Gerald Hannon, Ted Hand, Charles Harwood, Harry Hay, George Hodgman, Mitchell Ivers, Peter Judge, Ronald Judge, Dan Leach, Peter Lerangis, Richard La Rose, Frankie McGrattan, Peter McGrattan, Leo Mavrovitis, Arron Moses, Tom Murphy, Larry Peadson, Ronnie Peadson, David Ratcliffe, John Scott, Scott Skinner, Tom Spain, Dauna Staite, Ellen Staite, David Young, and Ian Young.

Richard Goldstein at *The Village Voice*, Peter Bloch at *Penthouse*, Max Allen of the Canadian Broadcasting Corporation, and Gary and Gail Provost gave Robin the kind of forums he needed to explore his ideas.

Diane Cleaver, Robin's tenacious literary agent, believed in Robin's talent from the start. Sadly, she did not live to see this book's completion. Heide Lange finished Diane's work with expertise and cheerful persistence.

Dawn Seferian, the editor who originally acquired Robin Hardy's book, nourished it as it developed, as did Will Lung.

I am very grateful to John Radziewicz, the Houghton Mifflin editor who brought his sharp and generous mind to bear in the book's arguments focus and vibrancy. His contribution was essential to this book. Jenna Terry helped shepherd the book to publication with great good will. Carl Walesa copyedited the book with care and engagement; Loren Isenberg and Lois Wasoff gave it a friendly and professional legal eye. Maya Baran and her assistant Whitney Peeling have brought dedication and inspiration to helping *The Crisis of Desire* reach a large readership.

I had support from many friends and helpful readers, including Peter Allen, William Berger, Jay Blotcher, Michael Bronski, Frank Browning, Spencer Cox, Charles Flowers, Larry Gross, Wesley Gibson, Fenton Johnson, Dan Lansner, Stephen Miller, Henry Scott, Michael Simmons, and Scott Tucker. Nicole Erhlich and Larry Gross provided crucial connections. Philip Gefter, Robin's good friend and mine, offered counsel and encouragement throughout, as did Jan Crawford and my parents. Stefan Lynch graciously agreed that his own story, and the story of his father Michael Lynch, should be told in these pages.

My lover Clay Williams has lived with the fact of this book as long as he has known me. His intellect, patience, and faith have given me the hope not only that I could complete this book but that all of us might rise to the vocation of desire — what Robin Hardy calls the brotherhood of lovers.

Cynthia Manson, Robin's steadfast friend and literary advisor extraordinaire, dedicated herself to ensuring that after his death his work would be published. I am deeply appreciative, and I know Robin's family is too.

Robin's brother Charles, his sister Michele, and his parents Bill and Jean encouraged in Robin the passion, independence of mind, and sense of justice he needed to write this book.

Robin's sister, Eloise Hardy, was one of his best friends. She was invaluable to me in guiding this book to life. Her spirit, openness, and hardy heart are reasons to admire her.

DAVID GROFF

INDEX

Robin Hardy (1952–1995) was a writer and AIDS activist. His essays and criticism appeared in the *Village Voice*, the *Advocate*, *Body Politic*, *Christopher Street*, and *Penthouse*. He received the PEN Center West Writers with AIDS Award for *The Crisis of Desire*.

After Hardy died in a hiking accident, his friend David Groff worked to complete his vision in this book. Groff's writing has been published in *Out, Poetry, Poz,* and *Men on Men 2.*